Learning
IN A
NEW
LANGUAGE

Learning
IN A
NEW LANGUAGE

A **Schoolwide** Approach to
Support K–8 **Emergent Bilinguals**

Lori Helman

ASCD

Alexandria, Virginia USA

1703 N. Beauregard St. • Alexandria, VA 22311-1714 USA
Phone: 800-933-2723 or 703-578-9600 • Fax: 703-575-5400
Website: www.ascd.org • E-mail: member@ascd.org
Author guidelines: www.ascd.org/write

Ranjit Sidhu, *Executive Director;* Stefani Roth, *Publisher;* Genny Ostertag, *Director, Content Acqui-sitions;* Susan Hills, *Acquisitions Editor;* Julie Houtz, *Director, Book Editing & Production;* Joy Scott Ressler, *Editor;* Judi Connelly, *Senior Art Director;* Masie Chong, *Graphic Designer;* Valerie Younkin, *Production Designer;* Kelly Marshall, *Interim Manager, Production Services;* Trinay Blake, *E-Publishing Specialist;* Isel Pizarro, *Production Specialist.*

All web links in this book are correct as of the publication date below but may have become inactive or otherwise modified since that time. If you notice a deactivated or changed link, please e-mail books@ascd.org with the words "Link Update" in the subject line. In your message, please specify the web link, the book title, and the page number on which the link appears.

PAPERBACK ISBN: 978-1-4166-2866-8   ASCD product #120015   n1/20
PDF E-BOOK ISBN: 978-1-4166-2868-2; see Books in Print for other formats.

Quantity discounts are available: e-mail programteam@ascd.org or call 800-933-2723, ext. 5773, or 703-575-5773. For desk copies, go to www.ascd.org/deskcopy.

Library of Congress Cataloging-in-Publication Data
Names: Helman, Lori, author.
Title: Learning in a new language: a schoolwide approach to support K–8 emergent bilinguals / by Lori Helman.
Description: Alexandria, VA: ASCD, 2020. | Includes bibliographical references and index.
Identifiers: LCCN 2019028429 | ISBN 9781416628668 (paperback) | ISBN 9781416628682 (pdf)
Subjects: LCSH: Linguistic minorities—Education (Elementary)—United States. | Linguistic minorities—Education (Middle school)—United States. | Limited English proficient students—United States. | Language arts—Correlation with content subjects—United States. | Second language acquisition—United States.
Classification: LCC LC3731 .H45 2020 | DDC 370.117—dc23
LC record available at https://lccn.loc.gov/2019028429

28 27 26 25 24 23 22 21 20   1 2 3 4 5 6 7 8 9 10 11 12

Learning IN A NEW LANGUAGE

An Urgent Call to Action

As an educational leader, you have many responsibilities entrusted to you by a range of stakeholders—the families and communities you serve, your students, the school staff, your organization's board or governing body, policymakers, and the greater community. These responsibilities range from basic management and safety to ensuring that all of your students have opportunities to become well prepared for college, career, and civic engagement. As times change, the responsibilities of school leaders continue to increase, and more information and strategies are needed to cultivate the success of an increasingly diverse population of students. It is in this context that *Learning in a New Language: A Schoolwide Approach to Support K–8 Emergent Bilinguals* has been written.

The book is designed to be a comprehensive and accessible resource for instructional leaders who work in multilingual communities with students who are acquiring English at school. The book brings together essential background information and evidence-based practical strategies into a one-stop reference for busy instructional leaders. The focus area of each chapter represents an aspect of educational reform that is often addressed in a full-length book. The purpose of this book, however, is to get to the heart of the topic quickly and present forthright solutions.

School leaders will vary in their background knowledge of the disciplinary content areas, the development of language and literacy, how to engage family members, cultural responsiveness, and schoolwide systems of support. This book is designed to provide foundational information in all these areas, with a focus on approaches that are effective for students learning in a new language and representing a variety of cultural communities. With the knowledge presented here, instructional leaders will be able to engage with educators and family members from a solid foundation of understanding. At the end of each chapter, online resources for further learning are shared to expand on the content.

This chapter serves as an introduction. To begin, it explores a few details about the cultural and linguistic diversity of students in K–8 classrooms in the United States and why recent demographic shifts call upon educators to enlarge and enhance their educational approaches. Students from historically marginalized communities—for example, those who speak languages other than academic English, are immigrants, have fewer economic resources, are people of color, are differently abled, or represent gender diverse or sexual minority populations—face obstacles to receiving equitable treatment in schools and classrooms. For this reason, a vision for equity is the backbone connecting each chapter of the book and is introduced here in the first chapter. The chapter also provides information about the terminology used throughout the book and previews the content of each chapter.

Why This Book Is Needed

Approximately 10 percent of K–8 public school students were identified as English language learners (ELLs) in the United States during the fall of 2015 (USDE/NCES, 2017). Greater percentages of ELL students attended school in California (21 percent), Texas (17 percent), and New Mexico (16 percent), and more students were likely to be in grades K–2 (~16 percent) than middle and high school (~4–8 percent; McFarland et al., 2018). A greater percentage of ELL students (~14 percent) lived in cities as compared to suburban areas (~9 percent) and towns or rural communities (~4–6 percent; McFarland et al., 2018). Dozens of languages are represented by multilingual students, but by far the language with the highest reported number of speakers in U.S. schools is Spanish

(77 percent), with Arabic, Chinese, and Vietnamese being the next most frequent (McFarland et al., 2018). Each student who brings a language other than English to school deserves to be accepted wholeheartedly into a community of learners there and to receive instruction that builds on their linguistic resources so that they have the potential to excel.

Being bilingual is an achievement that is valued universally and has numerous positive effects on individuals' lives. People who speak—and potentially are literate in—more than one language gain cognitive flexibility; may have improved executive functioning; are able to maintain relationships with extended family members; better understand people from different geographical, cultural, and linguistic groups; and are prized in the job market (Bialystok, 2007; Rodríguez, Carrasquillo, & Lee, 2014). With these benefits in mind, it is clear that schooling should *add* to a student's linguistic repertoire, not take away from it. Tailored approaches are presented throughout this book for learning about students' linguistic resources, using them to leverage learning in a new language, and working to sustain their bilingual capabilities. With a two-pronged strategy of valuing what students bring to school and using instructional methods that facilitate learning in a new language, students are both validated and provided with clear access to the curriculum.

The current reality in schools and classrooms does not usually reflect the best practices to support students from culturally and linguistically diverse backgrounds. Students are often viewed by what they lack rather than by what they possess. Family members who speak languages other than English are not frequently called upon to provide programmatic input or share what works with their children. For the most part, educators, who typically come from white and middle-class backgrounds, have not received enough preparation for teaching students who represent different races, social classes, and cultural and linguistic backgrounds. The result of these mismatches has been that students learning English at school are lagging behind in many metrics of educational success, including academic achievement, graduation rates, and career and college goals. The time is now to transform our schools into places that better serve students from traditionally marginalized communities. The plans laid out in this book present good starting points.

Focusing on Equity

Equity has been described as involving both fairness and inclusion. Equity is not the same as equality; students may need differing resources to achieve similar levels of success in their academic or social benchmarks (OECD, 2018). When a school's mission is equity, students who are not experiencing success are viewed as being underserved rather than possessing some form of deficit. Instructional leaders who promote educational equity seek to

- Identify who is not experiencing success within the local context.
- Collect related data to analyze and reflect on with school- and community-based stakeholders.
- Focus human and material resources to address inequities on-site and in the community.
- Move the equity vision to the forefront and lead the school community to set goals and action plans that result in social justice.
- Work in collaboration with families and communities to gather information, problem solve, monitor progress, and learn from outcomes.

Terminology Used

A number of terms are used throughout this book to characterize students' linguistic backgrounds and resources. Some of them are interchangeable, but they each hold a perspective or underlying value judgment. The sections that follow highlight the nuances of each term and explain why a given term might be used in particular cases.

Emergent Bilinguals

Students who bring a home language to school that is different from the language of instruction have the potential to be, and are becoming, bilingual. As they develop capabilities in the new language, their bilingualism is emerging. The term *emergent bilingual* views the student as reaching toward the enriched goal of possessing more than one language rather than using a term that positions the student as coming to school with deficits (e.g., English learner or limited proficient; García, Johnson, & Seltzer, 2017). Whenever possible throughout this book, *emergent bilingual* is used to describe students who are likely to have been described previously as English learners.

English Learner (EL) and English Language Learner (ELL)

The terms *English learner* (EL) and *English language learner* (ELL) also refer to students who come to school with a home language other than English and who require support in order to access the material and experience academic success. Because the EL or ELL label positions the student as *not* having something (deficit perspective), it feeds a negative stereotype and perhaps an instinct to blame the student or the student's family. These terms will be used only when quoting from research that has defined students with one of these labels.

Linguistically Diverse Students

The term *linguistically diverse students* describes students who bring languages or language variations that are not typically recognized or valued in the mainstream classroom where academic English is the language of instruction. Linguistically diverse students include not only those who speak a language other than English at home but also those who speak variations of English, such as African American English (AAE), Chicano English, Appalachian English, and others.

Bilingual/Multilingual Students

The term *bilingual* or *multilingual students* describes individuals who speak two or more languages or variations of a language—for example, a person who speaks English and Spanish or English, Spanish, and Nahuatl. Students who speak variations of English such as AAE and academic English also show multilingual skills and have the versatility to change codes depending on the people with whom they are communicating. Multilingual people often use interlanguage strategies (such as code meshing and translanguaging) when communicating with other multilinguals and may serve as interpreters when interacting with monolinguals who do not speak a common language.

Overview of Chapters

This book will work as a read-through from cover to cover or as a resource guide to pull from when information is needed about a particular topic. The chapters are designed to provide straightforward background information, examples of evidence-based practices, tips for where to start, and resources for further exploration. The idea is to give instructional leaders a "just right" amount of information to understand the big ideas and potential pathways to improving schooling for linguistically diverse students. No educational leader will be an expert in every area addressed in this book, nor should that be expected. Leading for inclusion means that progress comes from collaborative efforts where group energy has an exponential effect. The chapters in this book give instructional leaders the background they need to support the work of educators and specialists within a schoolwide context aimed at promoting equity for underserved students.

Chapter 2 focuses on the foundational goal of learning about and joining forces with family members and communities to support student learning. The ideas and actions outlined in this chapter are key to improving schooling for marginalized students because when there is alignment of students' in- and out-of-school experiences, students feel understood and supported. Family and community members have important information to share with educators about their priorities for schooling and what works best for their children.

Chapter 3 builds the foundation of big ideas used throughout the book: culturally and linguistically sustaining pedagogies, multitiered systems of support, and job-embedded professional learning. After these three frameworks are presented, example structures are highlighted that integrate the foundational principles in practical ways.

Chapter 4 examines how to make changes at the schoolwide level that increase inclusiveness for all students and center equity as the mission and vision on campus. The chapter describes how to look beyond school climate and do the deep work of creating a school culture that prioritizes just outcomes for all students.

Chapter 5 takes a focused look at a topic of critical importance to educators who work with emergent bilinguals—the development of oral language needed to be successful at school and how to nurture the teaching practices that enhance this development. The chapter provides educational leaders with specific types of teaching and language-learning interactions to look for as they visit classrooms.

Chapter 6 shines a spotlight on literacy learning in a new language and the best practices in instruction for emergent bilinguals. For busy leaders, the chapter provides enough information to gain a foothold in understanding literacy learning overall and also the general guiding principles that are applicable to any grade level for embedding language in more focused ways in the literacy classroom.

Chapter 7 turns to teaching and learning in content-area classrooms. Although many teachers in these classrooms do not have focused preparation in serving emergent bilingual students, they are called upon to make their curriculum accessible and engaging to them. The chapter suggests a number of ways to strengthen teaching behaviors and classroom environments so that they are more helpful to students learning through a new language.

Chapter 8 turns once again to a systemwide topic, facilitating professional learning that is connected to the vision and goals of the school and prioritizes equitable outcomes for all students. The chapter presents the components needed for powerful professional learning to occur and then describes how leaders can use structures such as professional learning communities, coaching, and data-based inquiry to support emergent bilinguals' success.

The final chapter and the Appendix provide straightforward continuous-improvement resources for identifying what is important to see and measure on the road to better serving emergent bilinguals and other linguistically diverse students. Chapter 9 suggests how a school leadership team might begin to assess its progress on equity goals using multiple measures. The Appendix presents a series of simple guides highlighting what an instructional leader might look for in the physical environment, interactions, and teaching behaviors in classrooms based on content presented throughout the book.

Fostering success with emergent bilinguals is a pressing challenge for all educational leaders, but with focus, persistence, and teamwork, it is one that can be accomplished. This book is designed to be a partner on this important mission.

Engaging with Linguistically Diverse Families and Communities

Schools are complex settings nested within larger communities that bring together a variety of people: students of various ages, their family members, educators, administrators, other staff and community members, volunteers, and more. The goal of this grand gathering is to "educate" the student, but what exactly that means depends on the stakeholders' perspectives, history, background experiences, and aspirations. Without a doubt, your school setting comprises people with diverse experiences, histories, and goals. Diversity also likely encompasses cultural backgrounds, linguistic backgrounds, differing economic resources, differences in citizenship documentation status, and parental education levels. Given this confluence of people with so many diverse characteristics, how can everyone form a cohesive school community and contribute to students' success? How can a multiplicity of voices be empowered to ensure that the school, and the community it is a part of, are working together to support the learning of their children?

A recent policy paper by the Global Family Research Project reinforced the critical role of families in education, highlighting the fact that children are awake for about 6,000 hours a year, and only about 1,000 of these are spent in school (Weiss, Lopez, & Caspe, 2018). Students learn both in and out of school; building on and valuing the roles that family members play in their children's education can have strong positive consequences for learners and schools, such as increased attendance, better bonding with teachers, higher academic achievement, increased success in meeting yearly progress goals, increased content relevance for students, higher teacher expectations for students, and better long-term educational outcomes (Berg, Melaville, & Blank, 2006; Blank, Melaville, & Shah, 2003; Dearing, Kreider, Simpkins, & Weiss, 2006; Ferguson, 2008; Henderson & Mapp, 2002; Marzano, 2003). However, old models of parent involvement have not equitably included the participation of all members of the school community. Family members who do not speak English, who are less familiar with the U.S. school system, whose work hours prevent them from visiting schools for meetings or assemblies, who do not have easy transportation to visit school, or who may be discouraged by their own personal traumatic school experiences need educators to structure ways for them to participate that can overcome some of these barriers. In effect, what is needed is a new way of creating and sustaining school-community engagement that is inclusive and enhances the success of every student. School leaders play an essential role in this work.

This chapter explores the why and how of more deeply including the families of emergent bilingual students in the life of a school and simultaneously involving the school staff more in the community. It is through this mutual goal orientation and relationship building that powerful partnerships can be built to support student learning (Mapp & Kuttner, 2013). Throughout the chapter, what it takes to set a foundation for collaboration between educators and families and community members is considered. A number of practices are highlighted that connect students' families and communities with educators and that help educators make their teaching more responsive to their students' lives and their communities' goals. The chapter concludes with a set of next steps for strengthening engagement among educators and the families and communities they serve.

A New Vision of Engagement

A quick survey of the literature on school-family-community partnerships highlights the changing nature of these relationships and the important role that site leaders play in a number of ways: a teaching role, a listening role, a connecting role, leading for democratic participation (Jennerjohn, 2017), or involvement as a community leader (Khalifa, 2012). To participate in an inclusive vision of school-family-community engagement, however, some foundational principles should first be addressed. These ideas involve examining what is needed for truly powerful collaboration to flourish.

Humanizing Family Engagement

Gallo (2017) studied the involvement of Mexican immigrant fathers in their children's education and, through this work, proposes a framework she calls *humanizing family engagement*, in which parent involvement is not viewed in a traditional, narrow manner (e.g., help with homework or school volunteerism), but, rather, as a broader vision of the ways families from marginalized communities provide resources and strength to their children. Instead of judging family members against a white and middle-class list of parent involvement expectations, Gallo (2017) invites educators to learn about the human strengths and capacities that diverse families share with their children and use this awareness to support their learning in the classroom.

Asset-Based Frame of Reference

For educators to work effectively in partnership with families and communities, it is important that they respect and value what students from all backgrounds bring with them to school—the *funds of knowledge* they have learned from families and members of their cultural or linguistic communities (González, Moll, & Amanti, 2005). A deficit-based frame of reference looks at students and identifies what they lack (e.g., English language skills), but an asset-based perspective sees that students bring many cultural and linguistic resources with them to school and that these are healthy for their development. Educator Anna

Jennerjohn describes visiting the home of a student, Daniel, prior to working on a literacy project with him. She got to see how the 6-year-old and his sister took turns unlocking their community mailbox to get the mail, how his dad had renovated their home, and how his parents' large wedding portrait was featured prominently in their living room, and she tried the typical Mexican cookie his mother served. As Anna left from her first visit to this neighborhood, Daniel's parents held hands as they walked her to the door and a man was selling watermelons to neighbors out of the back of his van. She felt that the visit was a helpful glimpse into Daniel's life at home that she could build on to support his writing at school. When educators uncover the assets and funds of knowledge students bring to school, not only can they structure relevant classroom learning experiences, but they can also communicate their acceptance of students and their families. Acceptance and appreciation are essential for building mutual trust.

Bidirectional Learning and Communication

A key pillar for constructing inclusive family engagement partnerships is that relationships and information flow back and forth, not taking shape in solely one direction or another. Two-way interaction means that educators communicate and share knowledge from school to home, for example, through written or electronic newsletters or parent meetings. In addition, families communicate and share knowledge with the school, for example, through regular feedback forms or educator listening sessions. In a traditional involvement model, children and their families learn through school and school-based activities. In a humanizing model, educators learn through home- and community-based activities as well. It is only through this bidirectional flow that partnership grows.

Examining Educator Dispositions

Old and stereotypical ways of viewing people from marginalized communities are still entrenched in school sites. Educators in many settings are predominantly white, middle class, and female, and often do not look anything like the people in the communities they serve. Most of these educators have English as a home language, and their students are much more likely to be multilingual than they are. These differences in background experiences can play a role in educators seeing students and their families as "different" or "other." Some myths that educators may hold include feeling that families "don't care" about their children's success at school or aren't "motivated" enough to make it to school for meetings and events. Following a group of immigrant students from diverse linguistic backgrounds through the elementary years, my colleagues and I never encountered a parent who didn't care or wasn't motivated to know more about their child's learning. However, factors such as working multiple jobs, not having transportation to school, not feeling welcome at school, and perhaps not speaking English well or having extensive literacy skills affected their participation with educators (Helman, Rogers, Frederick, & Struck, 2016). It is critical for school leaders to dig deeply into educator attitudes that can hamper student achievement by lowering expectations or not being able to find ways to connect classroom material with students' lives. Issues of race, language background, social class, and documentation status, among other identity markers, can influence educator and student actions both in and outside of the classroom (Blank, Berg, & Melaville, 2006; Datnow, Lasky, Stringfield, & Teddlie, 2005; Jones & Vagle, 2013; Khalifa, 2012; Valdés, 2001).

Built on Mutual Trust

Partnerships will not be powerful when collaborators cannot trust each other. Key to inclusive and productive school-family-community engagement is knowing that everyone is working toward common goals in ways that respect one another's contributions. Trust between educators and families and communities is developed over time and by actions, not simply words. Trust is built in many ways, including through personal relationships, shared values, working on common projects, and taking a role in community leadership (Henderson & Mapp, 2002; Khalifa, 2012).

Important elements of a new vision of school-family-community engagement include working to humanize interactions and perspectives related to the people who care for students, taking an asset-based perspective on what students bring to school, creating bidirectional learning opportunities, delving deeply into educator dispositions related to their students' identities, and building mutual trust through word and deed. The remainder of this chapter explores how to put these ideas into practice to support students from culturally and linguistically diverse communities.

Starting with Families

Creating a partnership with families and communities begins with listening and learning. Educators and educational leaders cannot create bridges from school to home to community and back unless they know a lot about all of these places. To gain insight into the values, joys, struggles, and aspirations of your school's families and communities, several key action strategies stand out: (1) listening to students, families, and community members informally and through structured activities; (2) venturing into the community; (3) collecting feedback regularly and persistently; and (4) structuring ways for family members to participate in school decision making. Figure 2.1 provides a graphic summary of the key approaches to gathering input from families and members of students' cultural and linguistic communities. This section explores specific examples of these strategies.

Engaging in Listening Activities

Family members care about their children and want them to succeed. Family members also know what works for their children in home and community settings and are generally happy to share their knowledge with school-based personnel who are willing to listen. So, the first step in setting up the school as a "listening place" is to cultivate a receptive and listening attitude with staff members. When a family member enters the school office, classroom, cafeteria, or library, how do staff respond? A listening attitude might involve putting on a friendly face, making an introduction, or asking how the staff person might help. If there is a language barrier, the staff person could find a bilingual person nearby to help. Or, if that is not possible, taking a positive attitude toward communicating with the visitor across languages—such as using gestures, artifacts, or whatever is known in the other person's language—always creates goodwill toward relationship building. Whether the school representative is the principal, receptionist, teacher, or custodian, being an attentive listener and documenting a family member's input is essential for learning about students. If barriers exist to listening at a given moment, it is important to find a way for the family member to share with someone else. A visitor who does not feel listened to is less likely to try again. By contrast, family members who find a listening attitude at school will continue to share and develop stronger connections with the people there. In turn, the school community will become more informed.

FIGURE 2.1
Action Strategies for Learning from Families and Communities

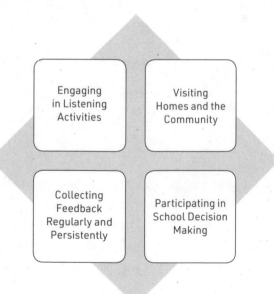

Engaging in Listening Activities

Visiting Homes and the Community

Collecting Feedback Regularly and Persistently

Participating in School Decision Making

There are a number of more formal ways to structure listening activities at school. Some schools have weekly meet-and-greet sessions with the principal for families to discuss what is on their minds. It is critical that community liaisons or other personnel who speak families' home languages be present at these gatherings. Teachers can be encouraged to divide "Back to School" nights and other parent meetings into two parts, saving half of the time to listen to family members' comments. When educational or community-based issues surface that are important to the school community, an open forum can be scheduled for family members to share their opinions. For example, a listening session could be set up with a focus on homework, bullying, or students' safety as they travel from school to home.

One way that Principal Dan Cavanaugh found to hear more from family members in his school community was to recruit them to take on positions at the school, such as crossing guards, health clerks, and office workers. When family members were embedded at school, there was an easy flow of information to and from the community. He also encouraged parents of current students to get their teaching licenses, and some later came back to the school as teachers. Whether formally or informally, listening to members of the school community fosters understanding among groups of stakeholders, strengthens relationships that can lead to trust building, and sets the stage for collaborating on real-world problems that have an influence on the well-being of children and their success at school.

Venturing into the Community

To really learn about the lives of students and their families outside of school, educators need to experience the area and the day-to-day activities of residents. For staff who don't live in the school neighborhood, a number of simple steps can be taken to get started. Staff who *do* live in the neighborhood can serve as guides for some of these activities:

- *Walk or take public transportation the way students do to learn about the landmarks; note the mix of commercial, residential, and natural spaces; and observe people along the way.* Write down interesting things you see and questions you have that you would like to talk about with residents.

- *Visit a local store where families from school shop.* Try to learn some new vocabulary—either words in students' home languages or English words you are unfamiliar with.
- *Eat out in some local restaurants that serve food from students' homelands.* Taste different things and remember the names of what you like so that you can share your experience with students at school.
- *Visit community events,* such as cultural fairs, music or dance performances, and sports events to become more knowledgeable and appreciative of the interests and activities of residents.
- *As you move around the community, notice signage and advertisements to get a sense of what topics are relevant to families' lives.*
- *If there are a few types of businesses in your school community where many family members work, visit and find out more about what the business does.* For example, students may have family members who are doctors with their own clinics, or business owners, work in agriculture related to specific crops, manufacture a certain product, work in construction, or support the leisure and hospitality industry. Becoming knowledgeable about the particulars of these jobs helps educators make connections to the daily lives of students' families that can be furthered at school.

One of the most recommended practices for educators to learn about students is for them to make *home visits* (Lin & Bates, 2010; Meyer & Mann, 2006). Making a home visit is often standard operating procedure to bridge awareness between home and school, set the stage for strong relationship building, and learn more about families' funds of knowledge that can be built on in the school setting. Educators are encouraged to arrange a visit to each child's home, with an interpreter if needed, and engage in a bidirectional conversation in which the educator shares goals for the school year and family members provide insight into their child's strengths and challenges. The educator spends most of the time in these visits listening and asking questions, such as these:

What can you tell me about your child's interests and strengths? How does your child learn best? What hopes do you have for your child this year at school? How can I be the best teacher for your child?

During a home visit, educators should be nonjudgmental and positive about how the family has provided a foundation for student learning. For example, if a parent apologizes for not being a fluent speaker of English, the educator should validate the importance of speaking in the home language. When family members teach children new words in the home language, they teach a new concept, and that concept can easily be transferred to English down the road at school. It is critical for family members to hear the message that speaking, singing, sharing stories, and other oral language activities in the home language are crucial for their children's future academic and social learning.

Although visiting each family in the class is the goal, home visits may not be possible in all cases. Educators can also meet with family members in the community—such as at a library, a park, a retail center, or another convenient location. Educators can ask to meet up with families before or after a sporting event they attend. Educators can also arrange to meet with more than one family at a time if that allows everyone to participate. When setting up a home visit was difficult for particular families in one of my research studies, I checked into local gathering places and found that many people often visited the public library in the neighborhood for a number of purposes. I was able to set up a time when three families could join me there for a conversation. The interaction felt nonthreatening and gave family members a chance to talk with one another as well as share with me. However home visits are set up, the important thing is for the educator to learn about the child and family, show appreciation for the part the family plays in success at school, begin to build a relationship that will sustain collaboration through the academic year, and gather ideas for how to support student learning based on the funds of knowledge the child brings from home.

Collecting Feedback Throughout the Year

A third strategy for learning about families is to gather their ideas and opinions throughout the school year. Typically, this data collection happens through surveys and questionnaires, focus groups, and interviews. At the beginning of each school year, educational leaders can construct a schoolwide survey that is fairly straightforward yet provides family members with an opportunity to share their priorities about the school program and how it can be improved. The survey can be laid out as a rating (e.g., "On a scale of 1–4, how important is this?"), a prioritization (e.g., "Put the following things in order of priority"), or a simple yes or no choice (e.g., "Should this be an important focus of our work at school this year?"). Surveys should be translated into all of the home languages of students' families and sent out automatically, not by special request. The survey should be sent out again midyear to gauge whether family members have revised their opinions or have new ideas for school improvement.

Classroom teachers and specialist teachers should be asked to send out brief questionnaires three times a year to families in their classrooms (fall, winter, spring). To reduce the risk of teachers feeling threatened, these questionnaires are only for their eyes and are not used by administrators for any accountability purposes. The questionnaires can be as simple as asking family members, *What is going well so far in our classroom for your child? What problems or challenges is your child experiencing? What next steps do you suggest?* Once again, the questionnaires should be translated into all home languages necessary, and teachers will need support to read forms that are completed in languages they don't speak. Families with limited literacy skills can be encouraged to share their opinions verbally. School staffs that have used this type of information gathering have found it a productive way to learn from family members and adjust their instruction in meaningful ways.

Focus groups and interviews are in-depth ways to gather information, perhaps around a specific topic or related to a group of students who are not flourishing at school. For example, a group of family members could be invited to school or a community location and asked to converse about how the school might increase participation at scheduled events or how upper-grade students might be supported to maintain their enthusiasm for checking out library books. Based on the needs that surface in the schoolwide survey, smaller group listening sessions can help provide a road map of potential solutions.

All of the listening, exploring, and inquiring activities presented in this section help educators better understand how school is working or not for their students, provide outlets for families to influence school structures and practices, and form a body of foundational knowledge that school-based personnel can use to anchor learning on the out-of-school knowledge that students bring from home.

Sharing About School

The bidirectional approach to school and family engagement involves both listening to the school community and providing family members with clear and useful information about how their children's school and classrooms function. This sharing should be delivered in a way that is respectful of the cultures, languages, and values of the community and that enables students to function well both in and outside of academic settings. For example, if educators have the attitude that only white, middle-class norms and academic English will serve students in their lives, they ignore the ways that bilingualism and the capacity to use a variety of linguistic codes enrich students' lives. Outside of school, students communicate in multiple ways with a range of family members, friends, and the public. The more languages and language variations they can access and the greater understanding they have of people from different cultures and backgrounds, the broader their reach and world will become. The last thing educators should do is attempt to erase the multilingual and multicultural capabilities that students bring to school.

For this reason, sharing *about* schooling and academic content should always be done in a humanizing and inclusive manner and should build on goals important to the school community. Figure 2.2 highlights some of the ways that traditional school meetings and events can become more responsive to students' cultural and linguistic backgrounds and not position the school as the sole holder of all knowledge that students need to learn.

Community liaisons are staff members whose job is to connect school with family members and help communicate important information in both directions. For example, a community liaison may support a teacher calling a family to set up a home visit or check on a student's absence. The community liaison may also field calls from family members about school events or share specific concerns or suggestions. Many of the ideas listed in this chapter can be facilitated with the help of an outgoing, bilingual community liaison who serves as a human bridge between groups of people. In a multilingual school community, it is important to find people who can serve in this role for all of the linguistic groups represented.

FIGURE 2.2
Enhancing Traditional School Events to Be More Responsive

Traditional School Event	Improving Cultural and Linguistic Responsiveness
Back-to-school night	• Provide child care • Use interpreters for languages the teacher does not speak • Translate handouls of information and use plenty of visual icons to clarify the message • Have time during the meeting for parents to share their ideas and goals
School orientation for new families	• For transnational families, explain some of the differences between U.S. schools and elsewhere in a nonjudgmental manner • Provide translated information with visuals • Use welcoming language and behavior • Demonstrate the information using artifacts and modeling (e.g., show some examples of book bags and supplies) • Encourage families to use and interact in their home languages • Seek out questions and leave plenty of wait time to hear them

(*continues*)

FIGURE 2.2

Enhancing Traditional School Events to Be More Responsive (*continued*)

Traditional School Event	Improving Cultural and Linguistic Responsiveness
Parent–teacher conferences	• Arrange for interpreters • Slow down and check frequently that parents understand what is being shared • Have artifacts and handouts to reinforce the information presented • Clearly explain the difference between progress toward standards and students' behavior or effort so that both can be discussed • Validate students' journey toward bilingualism • Save plenty of time for family members to share and ask questions • Consider holding conferences as home visits
Family literacy night	• Communicate that there is no one way to share a book or tell a story • Invite families to share about positive experiences with their children with songs, poems, stories, or riddles • Encourage use of the home language while engaging in literacy activities, including by discussing the book or summarizing what happened in the home language • Use culturally diverse literature • Create opportunities for children and their family members to read, write, and tell stories with one another based on topics of interest in the community • Model procedures for how parents can support children's use of school materials at home (e.g., doing word sorts, writing in a journal, or documenting their reading through a log) • Translate handouts of information and use plenty of visual icons to clarify the message
Curriculum nights (science, mathematics, art, etc.)	• Involve family members in hands-on learning with their children • Use interpreters for languages the teacher does not speak • Make connections between the content under discussion and the outside-of-school lives of students and their families • Bring in the voices of family members concerning their background experiences with the content area (e.g., *What have your experiences been in working with clay or seeing art made of clay?*) • Translate handouts of information and use plenty of visual icons to clarify the message

Joining Forces to Support Student Learning

So far in this chapter, the importance of making school-family engagement a humanizing experience, cultivating it by listening and learning in the community, and finding ways for educators to inform family members about schooling in clear and inclusive ways has been explored. This section delves into what it means for educators to work in partnership with families for student success. This idea is not a one-sided approach where one group tells the other what to do. Rather, ways to use collaboration to enhance outcomes for all stakeholders—in particular, the students—are considered.

All parents and caregivers want their children to be successful at school and in life, and they rely on educators to help make this happen. In turn, school personnel are much more successful when they work with family members and others in the community to support children both in and outside of school. Students are more successful when they sense cohesion between their school life and the outside world. This happens when students know that there is communication between home and school, when they believe that educators care about the health of their loved ones and communities, and when the school world sets high goals for them.

The first step in joining forces to support student learning is for educators to address issues of race, class, and language bias that they may hold consciously or unconsciously and that could negatively affect the expectations they have for students or their ability to partner with students' families. The Coalition for Community Schools advises leaders to "create opportunities for honest conversations about differences from the earliest stages of vision building" (Berg et al., 2006, p. ES-4). Not checking assumptions about groups of people in an open manner can lead to misunderstandings and cause a loss of trust. For this reason, norms should be set for working on school- and classroom-based projects that encourage everyone to ask questions and learn together in a respectful way. One such norm might state, "This is a safe place for learning about others, where we help one another overcome stereotypes."

As the school and community groups learn more about each other, real-life problems can be identified for everyone to work on together. For example, a school-based problem might be the lack of outdoor play equipment on campus or an interest in creating a school garden for science lessons. A community-based problem might relate to the safety of students walking home from school, the need for adult English classes, or lack of access to fresh produce in the neighborhood. Any number of issues could surface that might be used to forge a bond between school personnel and community members, improve the lives of students and their families, and enhance students' academic success. At times, school-community partnerships can take on a two-generation approach, such as the Children's Literature Project in California, through which families read and discussed books that were being read at school with their children (Arias & Morillo-Campbell, 2008). In this way, both parents and children learned together. In a study by Khalifa (2012), a principal who advocated for local causes in a marginalized community engendered trust and saw parents support school efforts in deeper and previously unseen ways.

Joining forces with families and communities is also critical at the classroom level. There are many ways for educators to build on students' funds of knowledge and involve family members in the learning community. The following list is just a starting point for teachers:

- During meetings early in the school year or at home visits, teachers ask family members what their jobs and talents are so that they have a sense of ways to involve them in class.
- New topics of study in class are introduced through content that is accessible to students and their family members. For example, when studying about life cycles in class, a team of 1st grade teachers decided to begin with strawberry plants, a crop that many families worked in locally (Morrison, 2017). Students were able to collect information about strawberries at home and in the community, and throughout the learning process both school and home were seen as sources of knowledge and venues for engaging with the material.

- Educators let family members know ahead of time when they are studying a new topic to see who has experience they might be willing to share informally.
- Children's literature is sought out that represents the cultural and linguistic backgrounds of students in class. In turn, personal or community-based challenges that the characters face can provide an opening for students to share more about their own lives (López-Robertson, 2017).

Classrooms can and should be welcoming places for family members to visit, whether simply to watch, to help out, or to take on a collaborative leadership role. Chapter 4 takes a deeper look at creating a welcoming environment at school. Knowing that a family member can come to help regularly is wonderful, but that is not always possible. Inviting family members to visit as their schedules allow is an important way to set the stage for inclusion and involvement.

Working together to help students learn and enrich the opportunities they have both in and outside of school is a long-term process that requires strong bonds among families, schools, and communities. Many books and brochures are available to guide leaders on this journey, and several options are included later in this chapter under "Resources for Further Learning." Regardless of the road map you use to plan for this essential work, the important thing to remember is that when communities talk together, learn from one another, and join forces to provide opportunities and support for students, everyone grows.

Tips for Strengthening Meaningful Family Engagement in Schools

Inclusive school-family-community engagement will take time, staff self-reflection, and intentional relationship building among stakeholders. The following ideas may help get your work started:

- *As described earlier in this chapter, set a goal for helping your school become a "listening place."* Collect data on how family members are treated on campus by shadowing them informally or asking for their feedback. Take your data back to staff and discuss ways to improve family members' comfort at school.

- *Create an expectation and structure for teachers to conduct home visits early on in the school year.* Provide material resources, such as interpreters, professional development time, and guidance for how to conduct the home visits. Build in time at staff meetings for teachers to discuss their experiences and what they learned through home visits and to collaboratively brainstorm opportunities to use students' funds of knowledge in their curriculum and classroom procedures.

- *Delve into deep-seated beliefs that staff on-site may have about people from racial, linguistic, socioeconomic, cultural, religious, and other marginalized groups that the school serves.* First steps for this work could include opening up conversations with staff about the values and experiences they acquired from their families and providing time for discussions in meetings to make connections to the values students bring from their homes. It is also helpful for community liaisons to have opportunities to share their insider knowledge about the families they know well and invite other staff to ask questions on a regular basis. The deep-seated work of identifying stereotypes that staff may hold or unintentional inequities that may be playing out on campus may be more productive if a facilitator from outside the building can guide the reflection. Give the process time and provide a safe environment for all to learn and begin to tackle head-on the stereotypes that negatively affect student learning and community engagement. This important topic is revisited at various points in Chapters 3, 4, and 8.

- *Revisit the cultural and linguistic responsiveness of the traditional family involvement activities that take place at your school to see where you might enhance them.* Use the suggestions in Figure 2.2 and think of additional ideas tailored to your school community.

- *Conduct surveys, questionnaires, interviews, focus groups, and meet-and-greets regularly* to better understand your school community's thoughts about the school program and how it could be improved.

- *Involve family members and community representatives in long-range planning for school improvement.* Set the vision collaboratively, hearing as many community voices as possible.
- *Work with district leaders to ensure that communications sent out to family members are clear, understandable, and consistent with messages coming from the school level.*

Summary

This chapter shined a spotlight on the importance of school-family-community partnerships and how they support student learning and successful schools. Whereas traditional parent involvement models did not open doors for most parents to participate, inclusive models aim to humanize educators' views of family members and identify the substantial resources they provide to support their children. A new vision of engagement is bidirectional and collaborative; staff learn about the funds of knowledge families have to offer and use these assets to tailor instruction in responsive ways in the school and classroom. The chapter highlighted a number of ways for educators to listen and learn from the community, seek out new experiences with community members, build trust, and share school-based information in clear and accessible ways. Educators are encouraged to join forces with families and communities to overcome real-world challenges and enact improvement projects that contribute to students' well-being and educational success.

Resources for Further Learning

There are many documents, organizational websites, and other resource materials to support you in creating a plan for working toward inclusive family engagement at your school site. Here are a few that you may find useful:

- **Toolkit of Resources for Engaging Families and the Community as Partners in Education.** This set of four documents from the Institute for Education Sciences guides leaders to: (1) build an understanding of family and community engagement; (2) build a cultural bridge; (3) build trusting relationships through communication; and (4) engage all in data conversations. For materials, including research, promising practices, tools, and resources, visit https://ies.ed.gov/ncee/edlabs/projects/project.asp?projectID= 4509.

- **Partners in Education: A Dual Capacity-Building Framework for Family-School Partnerships.** This archived document, created by Southwest Educational Development Laboratory, presents a research-based guide to designing family engagement for student success and developing capacity among educators and family members. For the framework, visit http://www.sedl.org/pubs/catalog/items/family132.html.
- **Global Family Research Project.** This nonprofit entrepreneurial organization supports family and community engagement practices that bolster students' success. Their website includes a variety of resources to build capacity in educators for doing this work and to fight against myths that may impede more robust parent involvement. Visit https://globalfrp.org/.
- **Colorín Colorado.** This website serves educators and families of emergent bilingual students with articles, tips, and recommended literature for parents and teachers; videos; and information about bilingualism and learning to read. Many materials are also available in Spanish. Visit http://www.colorincolorado.org/.

3

Essential Pieces of Program Improvement

Far-sighted educational leaders know that piling initiative after initiative and expectation after expectation on staff and students in a school community is overwhelming and leads to frustration and eventually maybe even burnout. Like blocks in a stacking game, eventually the pile will become unbalanced and topple over. In contrast, when decisions about school improvement processes are firmly anchored to the bedrock of fundamental principles that undergird the school's vision, efforts gain synergy and strengthen the collective mission. This chapter examines the solid core that upholds the strategies used to create equity for linguistically diverse students in the school change process. These fundamental principles include culturally and linguistically sustaining pedagogies, multitiered systems of support, and job-embedded professional learning, as illustrated in Figure 3.1. The figure highlights how the bedrock principles become established through contextualized professional learning that supports the innovative practices for which the school strives.

This chapter shares foundational knowledge called upon throughout the rest of the book. It begins with an explanation of the essential components of program improvement, providing a description and background information related to culturally and linguistically sustaining pedagogies, multitiered systems of support, and job-embedded professional learning. These three core frameworks are consolidated into a cohesive structure for building a responsive school, answering the question, *What culturally and linguistically sustaining actions could take place within a multitiered system of support and be supported by ongoing professional learning?* Several specific potential actions elucidate what this cohesiveness might look like. The chapter concludes with a sharing of follow-up resources for further exploration.

FIGURE 3.1
Fundamental Principles of Program Improvement

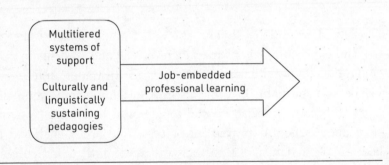

Culturally and Linguistically Sustaining Pedagogies

Most educators have heard the terms *culturally responsive teaching* or *culturally relevant pedagogy*. These concepts are based on the understanding that each person—whether an educator or a student—brings cultural ways of being to the school and classroom. What people learn from their families and communities shapes their expectations for other interactions and helps them interpret and engage with the world. Educators who are monolingual, English-speaking, white, and from middle-class backgrounds may not perceive that schooling itself is reflective of the norms related to these experiences. These educators might assume that all students learn in the same way and that expectations for students' and their families' participation, behavior, and motivation at school present themselves in universal ways. This belief ignores evidence from sociocultural and linguistic research that highlights the difficulties students may experience when their repertoires of practice—including discourse use in the home and community, cultural views and values, linguistic variation, and socialization patterns—collide with the often-unconscious values that operate in every aspect of the schooling process (Garcia, 1993; Gutierrez & Rogoff, 2003). For example, many students are raised in families that value interdependent actions, such as helping take care of younger siblings, contributing to the family income, or putting the family before other activities. When students who hold these interdependent value systems confront school expectations for "doing your own work" or competing against peers in class, this may lead to conflict because educators and students are operating with different world views (Au, 2016).

The collection of terms related to culturally responsive or culturally relevant teaching (CRT) is based on some shared assumptions and guides educators to enact a number of instructional approaches that facilitate access to the curriculum for students who hold diverse world views (Au, 2016; Gay, 2010; Ladson-Billings, 2009). Geneva Gay (2010) describes this approach as teaching *to* and *through* students' strengths. Figure 3.2, while not comprehensive, presents several foundational ideas on which CRT is based and how these ideas may take shape in preK–8 classrooms.

Emergent bilinguals represent culturally diverse populations and thus profit from CRT practices. They bring unique assets based on their language backgrounds as well, and it is for this reason that researchers have proposed a framework for the preparation of linguistically responsive teachers (Lucas & Villegas, 2010). In addition to the knowledge needed for CRT, teachers of linguistically diverse students must be prepared to understand and build on the languages students bring to school, apply key principles of language learning, and scaffold instruction for language learners (Helman, Ittner, & McMaster, in press; Lucas & Villegas, 2010). These culturally and linguistically responsive practices are highlighted throughout this book, especially in Chapters 5, 6, and 7.

FIGURE 3.2
Key Principles and Manifestations of CRT

CRT Principle	What It Might Look Like
A pluralist view of society: Students bring cultural strengths that deserve inclusion in the classroom and that serve them well outside of school.	• The classroom curriculum features people who represent many forms of diversity. • The school environment represents multiculturalism and multilingualism. • Students' out-of-school capabilities are used in their classroom activities and assignments.
A focus on equity: Some students are underserved by school systems and educators.	• Multiple forms of data are collected to identify which groups of students are or are not profiting from instruction at school. • School resources, both human and material, are prioritized for where there is a lack of equity. • Professional learning plans focus on building staff capacity to create equitable outcomes for students of all backgrounds.
Family contributions: Connections can be made between the curriculum and students' funds of knowledge.	• Educators gather information about what students learn and do in their homes through surveys, home visits, community meetings, and more. • Family members participate in classroom and schoolwide events where their strengths are shared and acknowledged. • Units of study, texts, and assignments build on the background knowledge that students bring with them from home.
Empowerment and high expectations: Students endeavor for academic success, multicultural competence, and critical thinking.	• Students from all demographic groups at school participate in enrichment programs, such as GATE (gifted education) and after-school clubs and work with high-quality teachers. • Students, instead of attempting to "erase" their home or out-of-school identities, are able to acknowledge and express them at school. • The curriculum is not designed to be rote acquisition; students have many opportunities to work on projects that critique social inequities affecting their lives and communities and work for change.

More recently, the term CRT has been transformed to explicitly highlight the goal of *sustaining* students' languages, literacies, and cultures (culturally sustaining pedagogy; Paris, 2012). In turn, educators, researchers, and policymakers have taken up the descriptor *culturally and linguistically sustaining pedagogy* (CLSP), built on the foundations of CRT and linguistically responsive practices. As a bedrock principle for this book, CLSP means that educators value the cultures, languages, experiences, and family assets that students bring to school; see them as important to the success of students and our pluralistic society; and work to sustain these diverse capabilities through schooling. For each aspect of schooling—what to teach, goal setting, relationship building, or measurement of accomplishments—educators must reflect on how the outcome affects cultural and linguistic sustainment. Only when educators take this principle to heart will students experience the validation, support, and enrichment they deserve.

Multitiered Systems of Support

The second key framework that undergirds this book is a systematic approach for identifying and serving students in an ongoing manner as they acquire the expected academic and social-emotional skills of their grade levels. This framework is best known as a *multitiered system of support* or MTSS. Through an MTSS structure, educational entities such as schools, districts, or statewide bodies outline procedures for ensuring that students receive the instruction they need to successfully reach grade-level benchmarks. MTSS (through a Response to Intervention/ RTI approach) delineates several layers of instructional support: Tier 1 is the universal experience that all students have in their regular classrooms; Tier 2 is the supplemental support provided to students who, with general classroom instruction alone, are not yet experiencing success, perhaps 15–20 percent of a classroom population; Tier 3 is a more individualized and intensive level of support needed for students who are not making good gains even with Tier 2 support, frequently estimated at 5 percent of a classroom population (Shapiro, n.d.).

MTSS is a proactive model that helps educators understand which students require added support at school without waiting for summative evaluations of their progress, such as year-end test scores. MTSS uses ongoing assessments of student learning and data-based decision making to ensure that the core classroom instruction (Tier 1) is as effective as possible for all students. When students need extra support, educators are guided to provide further small-group instruction (Tier 2) that will help students bridge to the classroom curricula and goals. This additional instruction might be provided within the classroom setting by teachers or specialists, or outside of the classroom in supplementary ways. While students receive Tier 2 support, frequent assessments of their learning take place to make sure the interventions are having their expected effects.

Quality Core Instruction

The majority of students spend most of their school day in their general education classroom participating in learning activities alongside a group of peers. For this reason, all students deserve high-quality experiences that will help them develop academic and social proficiencies from the start in their home classroom. If there is not effective instruction at the universal (Tier 1) level, no school will have the resources to accommodate that need with supplementary interventions (Burns & Gibbons, 2012; Gibbons, Brown, & Niebling, 2019).

How can a school evaluate whether the core classroom instruction is helping the greatest number of students reach state and district academic and social-emotional goals? The Center on Response to Intervention has listed the following items on its self-assessment rubric (American Institutes for Research, 2014):

- *Research-based curriculum materials.* How and to what extent was the research behind the school's curriculum materials a focus for their selection?
- *Within and across grade levels articulation of teaching and learning.* What processes are used to ensure consistency of instruction for students in the same grade level and coherence from grade to grade?
- *Differentiation of instruction.* How are student assessment data, including informal teacher assessments and understandings of students' languages and cultures, consistently used to address student learning needs?

- *Focus on learning standards*. To what extent and how are core curricula, instructional materials, models of teaching, and professional learning aligned to state standards?
- *Students exceeding benchmarks*. What programs and activities are available beyond core instruction for students who are working above grade level?

The Path to Reading Excellence in School Sites (PRESS, 2016) research project developed a set of quality indicators for core instruction in literacy that included the following key elements:

- Instruction is connected and meaningful (e.g., students engage in actual reading and writing practices, students see connection of activities to the real world).
- Instruction is systematic and explicit (e.g., material is comprehensible, and students receive feedback on their performance).
- Teaching practices are research based (e.g., there is an identifiable core element for instruction, and students receive adequate time and practice on the concept).
- Instruction is at student's level (e.g., teacher differentiates according to informal assessments).
- Instruction is tailored for English learners (e.g., teacher clarifies unknown vocabulary and models language structures).

The classroom environment is a key partner in quality core instruction as well. Some signs of quality in the literacy classroom include the access students have to information and tools, the use of a variety of texts and evidence that they are being used on a regular basis in class, and technology tools for students to use in reading and writing (PRESS, 2016). Literacy instruction is examined in greater depth in Chapter 6. Multiple tools to focus classroom observations of instruction and the learning environment are included in easy-to-use formats in the Appendix.

Use of Data for Problem Solving

Another pillar of MTSS is the systematic use of a variety of types of data to manage resources that support student learning. Typically, a school that operates within an MTSS framework collects the following data:

- *A universal screener*. Given to all students at set points in the school year to identify who needs extra support to be successful on grade-level objectives.
- *Diagnostic assessments*. Used to identify specific areas within the learning continuum that students need to work on.
- *Progress monitoring*. Assessments given to students receiving supplementary instruction or intervention.

A school that uses research-based assessment tools at regular intervals and confirms decisions about student learning with multiple measures has set in place a structure for being responsive to students, as opposed to waiting for them to fail. Also needed are structures with which to analyze the data so that decisions can be made for providing students with further support. This typically happens through collaborative meetings, such as those between grade-level data teams, leadership teams, professional learning communities (PLCs), and child study teams.

Tiered Interventions

Once data on student learning have been collected and analyzed, the MTSS framework provides a structure for ensuring that students who are not yet successful on grade-level benchmarks get additional help. To begin, if screening measures provide evidence that more than half of students within a given classroom need extra support, it is important that a classwide approach to intervention be implemented first. Classwide interventions deliver focused supplemental instruction to the whole class for 10–12 days and can reduce the need for a majority of students to participate in Tier 2 interventions later (Burns, Pulles, Helman, & McComas, 2016). They can also steer core instruction in a direction that will better help students acquire standards-based content in particular classrooms. If fewer than half of the students in a class need supplementary instruction or, following a classwide intervention that has reduced the number of students who need intervention to a more manageable number, students who could use focused support in an identified area should receive additional small-group instruction. For example, students who are not meeting the benchmark standard in their reading development (e.g., letter-sound knowledge or reading a grade-level passage) should be given a diagnostic assessment and then receive instruction in the identified area(s) of need. Each week of supplementary intervention, their progress is monitored to look for growth. If progress is not evident, the intervention should be adapted so that it is effective with the students.

Schools have used a variety of ways to support small-group tiered interventions on-site. The classroom teacher can lead small-group interventions while a co-teacher or assistant manages an activity for students who do not need the intervention. Specialist teachers can work with small groups of students on identified needs at a time that does not take them away from core academic subjects. Teams of educators can work together to instruct students collaboratively across the grade level, enabling one or more of the teachers to provide supplementary instruction to students who need the support in small groups. Some schools set up a time each day for students to be part of a learning experience to support their continued progress; in this case, all students go somewhere, and students receiving Tier 2 instruction go to their small-group intervention. Figuring out the details of how to structure supplementary small-group instruction is a context-based process. Each school has human, material, and space resources that will enable or constrain its options. Only by engaging in the details for how to make it happen, however, will schools enable students to grow along with their peers without falling behind.

The next component in the tiered system is for intensive and individualized intervention (Tier 3). This level of intervention is called for when small-group, focused interventions based on students' diagnosed needs are not helping students progress. Once again, it is critical that the interventions used be evidence-based, delivered by a knowledgeable professional, and allow the teacher to adjust instruction to match students' needs. It is also important that intensive intervention be cohesive with the instruction students receive in their general education classroom. For example, if two different mathematics approaches or sequences of phonics skills are used in the classroom and in intervention, students are likely to become confused and have more difficulty acquiring the concepts.

Some educators think that data-based and culturally and linguistically sustaining approaches are at odds with each other, but many people are working to ensure that: (1) CLSP uses data to ensure that no student "falls through the cracks" in meeting learning goals; and (2) their MTSS framework incorporates the perspectives of culturally and linguistically diverse students and their families when planning and delivering instructional support. Later in this chapter, several examples of initiatives that blend MTSS with CLSP will be explored.

Job-Embedded Professional Learning

The final principle highlighted in this book to guide work toward equity for emergent bilinguals is that professional learning for sustainable school improvement does not happen through "once and done" workshops for educators or in isolation, but takes place over time in dialogue with others and situated in the meaningful problems of practice at particular school sites (Raphael, Vasquez, Fortune, Gavelek, & Au, 2014). Lieberman and Miller (2014) call this *professional learning as growth in practice* and note that it involves extended professional interaction and inquiry, relies on both inside-the-school and outside expert knowledge, focuses on issues of importance to school goals, and encourages the thoughtful and critical reflection and analysis of participants. When professional development becomes something that is done *to* educators and in the primary interest of increasing test scores, authentic improvement of schooling for diverse students is unlikely to take hold. However, when student learning, instead of simply accountability for state test results, becomes the focus, educators and school leaders can construct diverse professional learning opportunities that allow them to use their knowledge of teaching and the needs of students in their community to make the school's vision closer to a reality (Firestone & Mangin, 2014).

To get a picture of how this situated, or job-embedded, professional learning takes shape, consider some of the following approaches that are highlighted throughout this book. Each of these involves collaborative learning over an extended time period and is centered around the dilemmas confronting educators in their specific schools. For example:

- Data analysis and supplementary student support planning meetings
- Professional learning communities
- Instructional coaching
- Lesson preparation, study, and analysis of student work
- Co-teaching
- Seeking solutions through action research
- Professional book clubs with application to practice
- Grade-level and schoolwide curriculum mapping and coordination
- Collaborative assessment of student work
- Learning through educational networks (e.g., writing projects or online networks)
- Community partnerships for social improvement

Many of these approaches are described in Chapter 8, and others emerge in various spots throughout the book. The bedrock principle, as illustrated in Figure 3.1, is that job-embedded professional learning is the vehicle that will enable culturally and linguistically sustaining practices within an MTSS structure to gain momentum and become prevalent throughout the educational community.

Example Structures and Strategies That Build on the Three Frameworks

This section will briefly explore several examples of what it might look like for a school community to implement culturally and linguistically sustaining practices within an MTSS structure. These illustrations are by no means all encompassing, but they will likely be good starting points or spark additional ideas about initiatives or actions a school community might take to move forward on its vision for equity.

Integrate CLSP Perspectives into the MTSS Framework

Many educational leaders who attempt to use basic MTSS structures in their multilingual and multicultural school communities arrive at a point where they feel something is missing. The MTSS framework on paper seems unidimensional (numbers on assessment data records, percentages of students meeting or exceeding benchmarks, etc.) and does not seem to reflect the richness and depth of what students bring to school and learn there. Over time, these leaders turn to CLSP to better understand the deep innovation that will be needed to better serve diverse students. To avoid this piecemeal approach, leaders get a head start by ensuring that the MTSS framework they implement centrally positions issues of diversity and equity. For example, educator and researcher Anne Ittner (2017) found that using multiple measures to monitor progress for emergent bilinguals more thoroughly identified the effectiveness of the support. By using student literacy profiles, informal reading inventories (IRIs), oral language rubrics, and anecdotal data, teams of educators discovered new ways to learn about students' language and literacy growth. Previously, the English learner (EL) teacher had not reviewed IRIs and the general education teachers had not examined oral language rubrics (Ittner, 2017). Adding a linguistic lens to supporting students facilitated an MTSS process that more accurately and comprehensively addressed student diversity.

Two examples of this integrated perspective come from the state of Wisconsin and the World-Class Instructional Design and Assessment (WIDA) Consortium. Goals for Wisconsin's model of an equitable MTSS framework are to ensure that services and resources are provided to every learner based on need. Their continuous improvement model puts equity at the center, surrounded by the strategic use of data, quality instruction, and collaboration. These central goals are supported through engagement with the community, shared leadership, the use of evidence-based practices, and a positive school culture (see www.wisconsinrticenter.org/school-implementation/overview-equitable-multi-level-system-support/

for further information). The WIDA Consortium (2013) has developed an MTSS framework guiding implementation for emergent bilinguals. The framework positions bilingual and English language instruction directly into the three-tiered model; describes necessary conditions for the framework to be successful for language learners; and clearly outlines factors that affect students' progress, appropriate assessment, and ways to support learners with exceptionalities (WIDA, 2013). This framework and other online resources can serve as useful guides for integrating CLSP understandings into an MTSS structure.

Use Culturally Sustaining Assessment and Goal Setting

As described earlier in this chapter, regular screening and progress monitoring assessments are critical for identifying which students may need extra support to be successful in reaching grade-level benchmarks. If the assessments used are not validated for diverse populations, however, the data will not be very useful and may underestimate what students are able to do. Educators must look closely at assessments (this can be an excellent focus for collaborative professional learning) to make sure they do not demonstrate bias against students because of their cultural backgrounds and values, socioeconomic resources, or language variation. In addition, multiple measures of student performance should be collected before any high-stakes decisions are made for individual students.

To maintain high expectations for all students, goals should also be set and measured concerning multilingual proficiencies. As the saying goes, "What gets measured gets done." If progress in language development and literacy in a home language is not documented or celebrated, it is not likely to be an important component in sustaining multilingual capabilities.

Involve Families in Data Analysis and Strategic Planning

Chapter 2 examined ways to increase the voices of families for sharing information about their children and setting the school vision. When MTSS becomes a guiding framework for school improvement, it is crucial that family members understand how the system works and what the data mean. To do this, educators must learn how to present and discuss data on student learning clearly and consistently with nonprofessionals. Community engagement professional and researcher María Paredes (2010) describes an innovative approach her district uses to share data at parent-teacher conferences. Teachers are supported to conduct parent-team meetings and individual conferences with family members where aggregate classroom performance data are shared, along with data for the individual student. Parents help set 60-day goals for student learning, and data are tracked over time to show how the child is progressing at different points in the year (Paredes, 2010; see videos at www.youtube.com/user/MariaParedesZ). Additional resources to help educators create plans for how they might inform family members about their children's progress on key learning goals, help them understand what the data mean, and provide guidance on resources that can support further growth in the area (Weiss & Lopez, 2011) can be accessed online at www.schoolcommunitynetwork.org/downloads/FACEHandbook.pdf. Specific professional learning activities that provide guidance on engaging family members in data conversations are available at https://ies.ed.gov/ncee/edlabs/projects/project.asp?projectID=4509.

Create an Equity Team

Your school is likely to have a leadership team or a school improvement team; however, explicitly naming a collaborative action committee that centers work around equity on campus can have powerful effects. This team can do some or all of the following:

- Study and propose solutions relating to disparities in student achievement on campus.
- Collect data on CLSP practices in use.
- Foster leadership development and professional learning on CLSP.
- Structure conversations about social justice in education.

As director of teaching and learning, Kari Ross made intentional efforts to include teachers of color in the district's curriculum design process and professional learning leadership groups. She noted,

"As a white woman, I have so many blind spots and need other perspectives to hear about what I don't know and haven't experienced. As I continue to work on my understanding of equity and the impact of implicit bias, I better understand how important it is to sustain relationships with people who offer critical and varied perspectives on the work of educating our learners. That way, we can build on the strengths and examine the possibilities when our plans do not result in success for each and every learner in the way we had intended."

See https://educationnorthwest.org/resources/equity-leadership-team-protocol for a protocol to support the work of an equity leadership team.

Promote Opportunities for Student Self-Determination

The use of quantitative data to represent student achievement can become a disempowering experience to many stakeholders if done improperly. Students may come to see themselves as a letter or number in their reading groups or a "below grade level" student in other subjects. Data should not be used to label or constrain students but should help them, their families, and their teachers work toward increased competency. As often as possible and in many diverse ways, students should be empowered to create goals for themselves, document their progress toward these goals, and celebrate their successes. Educator and researcher Donald Bear describes having students select *how* they will show they learned the content of a standard, giving students opportunities to self-assess their completed projects and provide input into grading and a chance to improve their work to get a better score. Instructional actions that lead to increased feelings of empowerment and self-determination may include the following:

- Goal-setting conferences with teachers
- Participation in support groups aimed at accomplishing an important objective
- Choice of instructional materials or topics of study in class
- Work on collaboratively selected community service projects

- Conducting inquiry projects and creating products to share using digital media
- Ongoing self-assessment relating to grade level, content area, or personal goals
- Reflection portfolios to share with teachers and families
- Documenting milestones toward biliteracy
- Being able to show progress through demonstration of mastery

Summary

This chapter built a foundation of key principles that are called upon in each chapter—culturally and linguistically sustaining pedagogy (CLSP), multitiered systems of support (MTSS), and job-embedded professional learning. These bedrock theories might take shape by integrating CLSP perspectives into the MTSS framework, using culturally sustaining assessment and goal setting, involving families in data analysis and strategic planning, creating an equity team, or promoting opportunities for student self-determination. These three essential programs can be integrated to create cohesiveness and synergy for building the school's equity agenda.

Resources for Further Learning

Resources on CLSP

Visit some of the following websites to learn more about culturally and linguistically sustaining educational practices:

- **Edutopia—Culturally Responsive Teaching.** Visit https://www. edutopia.org/topic/culturally-responsive-teaching.
- **Harvard Graduate School of Education—Linguistically Responsive Teachers.** Visit https://www.gse.harvard.edu/news/uk/ 18/04/linguistically-responsive-teachers.

- IES/REL—**Culturally Responsive Education, Best Practices and Supports.** Visit https://ies.ed.gov/ncee/edlabs/regions/mid-west/blogs/culturally-responsive-instruction-best-practices.aspx.

Resources on MTSS

The following websites provide helpful background information and guidance for implementing multitiered systems of support:

- **American Institutes for Research—Center on Response to Intervention.** Visit https://www.rti4success.org/.
- **Path to Reading Excellence in School Sites (PRESS).** Visit https://presscommunity.org/.
- **Office of Superintendent of Public Instruction.** Visit https://www.k12.wa.us/multi-tiered-system-supports-mtss/mtss-resources.

4

Creating Inclusive Schoolwide Structures and Environments

Education professionals can certainly agree on one thing—being an effective site leader is a complex undertaking, requires skills in a broad range of areas, and never lets up. This chapter will examine the ways that educational leaders work with school personnel, families, communities, and other stakeholders to create and maintain a physical environment and school culture that foster success for all students and, in particular, for emergent bilingual students. A quick peek at the *Professional Standards for Educational Leaders 2015* highlights several areas relevant to this chapter's focus (National Policy Board for Educational Administration [NPBEA], 2015, pp. 11–13):

- 3.a. Ensure that each student is treated fairly, respectfully, and with an understanding of each student's culture and context.
- 3.d. Develop student policies and address student misconduct in a positive, fair, and unbiased manner.
- 3.e. Confront and alter institutional biases of student marginalization, deficit-based schooling, and low expectations associated

with race, class, culture and language, gender and sexual orientation, and disability or special status.

- 5.a. Build and maintain a safe, caring, and healthy school environment that meets the academic, social, emotional, and physical needs of each student.
- 5.b. Create and sustain a school environment in which each student is known, accepted and valued, trusted and respected, cared for, and encouraged to be an active and responsible member of the school community.
- 5.f. Infuse the school's learning environment with the cultures and languages of the school's community.

Though only a portion of the total NPBEA standards, the aforementioned items highlight some of the many roles that educational leaders have in establishing schoolwide norms and environments that lead to academic achievement for students from marginalized communities.

This chapter focuses on the physical and social-emotional environments throughout a school that lead to high expectations and provide support for students learning in a new language. The chapter builds on ideas from Chapter 2, highlighting inclusive school-family-community engagement, and calls upon the culturally sustaining framework presented in Chapter 3. This chapter takes a deep look at what inclusion, safety, representation, and empowerment look and feel like for the clients at school—students and their families. It first explores some of the visible elements that demonstrate inclusion. Next, it delves into how systems that lead to equity and positive interactions on-site can become part of the culture of a school, make inclusion visible, and be enacted in the daily work of all members of the school community.

How an Inclusive School Climate Is Created

Many people describe school climate as a feeling they get when they walk in the door of the building. Does the place feel safe, comfortable, happy, active, austere, disorganized, welcoming, or *what strikes the visitor*? Depending on a person's background experiences and identities, the same place might evoke different responses. For example, one person walking into a beautifully updated and clean hospital may feel comfort and relief, while another, who holds traumatic memories based on hospital experiences or does not understand the language being used, may feel discomfort and fright. Creating an inclusive space at school for students, family and community members, staff, and others emanates from the physical environment, expectations within the social environment, and the overt and subtle ways that people interact with one another.

The Physical Environment

Not every school will have the same level of funding to support the purchase of furniture, technology, classroom supplies, and other resources, but it will be evident immediately upon entering a school if it is being cared for responsibly. In a school with clear norms, a strong feeling of ownership, and follow-through related to individual accountability, a visitor is likely to see staff and students being considerate of the physical environment—cleaning up spills, picking up trash in the hallways, adjusting papers that have fallen off the wall, and so on. The walls reflect messages aimed at informing or inspiring the community: What are recent highlights of school events? What interpersonal norms is everyone expected to follow? What are students at different grade levels learning? How does students' artistic work demonstrate beauty and creativity? These ideas and more should be evident in artifacts of student work or photographs visitors see when walking down the hallways of school and in common rooms.

To help visitors find their way around campus, signs should be posted directing them to key locations such as the school office, library, and cafeteria. Room numbers should be clearly labeled, along with the names of teachers and support staff. Directions and signs should be translated into the home languages of students' families, especially if the script used in their language is not the Roman alphabet (e.g., Chinese or Arabic).

Cultural and geographic diversity should be represented visually throughout the school. Some educational leaders do this by creating an inclusive mural highlighting places around the globe that students come from or showing the flags of these countries. Others have displayed alphabets or number lines featuring photographs that represent people of different backgrounds. Traditional decorations from specific cultures can be used to bring color and festivity to the school's walls—for example, *papel picado* from Mexico or murals based on African design patterns. Bulletin boards might feature cultural artifacts loaned from families or community-based organizations or show photographs of cultural events taking place in and out of school that involve student participation.

In an ideal environment, diversity is represented throughout the school. Signs underscore the benefits of knowing more than one language, and opportunities to work toward bilingualism or multilingualism, such as displays of students who have taken steps toward a biliteracy accomplishment, are evident. In addition to translations of directions and other procedural language, inspirational quotes, student writing, books and magazines, and art demonstrate languages other than English. A walk down the hallway or through a common space on campus feels like a linguistic and cultural learning experience. When students engage with the environment, they see mirrors of themselves and also windows into the lives of people who come from different backgrounds (Bishop, 1990). An observation guide highlighting aspects of the physical environment that support inclusion is included in the Appendix (Figure A.3).

The Social Environment

Taking a step deeper into creating inclusivity on campus involves considering the ways that educational leaders, students, staff, families, and community members interact. What norms and procedures guide these interactions so that students feel that school is a safe place to show themselves and their aspirations and that they will be given support for their learning? The foundation begins with the deep work that educational leaders do to create a mission and vision statement for the school. This vision, in turn, guides every aspect of the norms and daily work on campus. Figure 4.1 highlights a number of essential topics to be addressed when creating a culturally and linguistically inclusive vision statement to support positive relations and address equity issues such as those referenced in the NPBEA standards.

The information in Figure 4.1 uncovers some of the equity issues that may exist on a school campus. After considering these key areas, educational leaders can structure a visioning process that involves and informs all stakeholders—students, family members, staff, and the school community. Once established, the vision should be specific enough to hold everyone accountable. In other words, it is not enough to say "all students will succeed." The vision should highlight how equity of opportunity leads to accomplishment and call out how inequities will be overcome. This may involve the use of phrases such as "staff, students, and community members work across languages and backgrounds" or "a diverse community where everyone belongs and feels safe" or "promoting equity and inclusion" or "building on the unique strengths of the school community." Resources to support the important work of cocreating a school vision are included at the end of this chapter.

Once the school vision has been jointly created, it should shine through all aspects of school life. For example, the vision should be evident to family members and others when they visit school, participate in school activities, or receive written communications from school. A sample set of norms for a primary grade classroom might call on everyone to "Work together, listen to others, help one another to learn." In an upper grade or middle school classroom, norms might include "Respect for others, making your best effort, and no put-downs." Many classrooms also have signs highlighting how important making mistakes is to learning (e.g., "No one learns [succeeds/invents/triumphs, etc.] without trying and making mistakes"). This type of inspirational quote can be referenced consistently in class to encourage students to learn and grow together, instead of noticing one another's errors—including when they don't know a word in English or have difficulty with pronunciation. Students should know what the vision of the school encompasses, as well as what their personal roles are in upholding these values. The following is a brief list of some of the ways an inclusive and equity-based school vision might become evident:

- Schoolwide norms emphasize conflict resolution that is respectful of different cultures.
- Demeaning comments, jokes, and threats to students' physical and emotional well-being are not tolerated, including those based on students' English language capabilities.
- Multilingualism is celebrated. "English-only" policies are not supported either explicitly or implicitly.
- Schoolwide and classroom norms and procedures are understandable, maintain coherence with the schoolwide vision, and are put into effect in clear ways.
- Family members are called upon to help bridge cultural misunderstandings that may be causing dilemmas for students and staff at school.
- Students participate in diversity awareness experiences that help them learn about others' cultures, languages, and backgrounds.
- Staff use data to examine inequities in disciplinary actions, participation in enrichment classes, and progress in academic and nonacademic areas of schooling.
- Students are recognized for their role in upholding the inclusive vision of the school, perhaps by being given conflict-resolution leadership roles, being featured in stories in school newspapers, or receiving awards for demonstrating exemplary skills in areas such as mediation, team building, cross-cultural communication, or mentorship of a younger student.

Developing Relationships

I asked a principal with whom I had worked for many years how he had been so successful developing relationships with students at our elementary school. He immediately responded, "Learn their names!" He described a process he called "adopting the kindergarten," in which he would spend as much time as possible with the newest students on campus, getting to know the children and, if possible, their parents. This investment of time paid off over the years as the relationships remained strong throughout the students' and their families' time at the school. He had many other strategies for getting to know new enrollees

FIGURE 4.1

Centering Inclusiveness in the School Vision

Students' Identities and Background Experiences

- *Explicitly consider areas of diversity in your school community, such as languages or language variations spoken, cultural backgrounds, religious identities, differing levels of families' economic resources and employment, families' documentation status and security of housing, gender identities, special learning needs, or physical challenges.*
- *How informed about and accepting of these differences in the school community are staff members?*
- *How informed and accepting of these differences in the school community are students?*
- *What does adapting to diversity and creating a safe and equitable space for all students require in the context of your school?*

Belonging and Equity of Participation

- *Are there barriers to equal participation in classroom and school programs because of students' language skills, physical or cognitive challenges, economic resources, or other identity markers?*
- *Do family members experience barriers to contributing to school because of their language skills, economic resources, or other identity markers?*
- *Do students from certain demographic groups experience school discipline or punishment differentially, including by being excluded from learning settings (Morris & Perry, 2016)?*
- *How well prepared are staff members to better understand and develop trusting relationships with students from backgrounds different from their own?*

High Expectations

- *Data on multiple measures should document where students are in their academic, linguistic, and social learning journeys regardless of their demographic identifiers or background experiences. Each student should be supported to demonstrate accomplishment in these areas based on state and local standards, the aspirations of their families, and their own goals.*
- *Are there barriers to enrichment opportunities such as "gifted and talented" programs at school because of students' linguistic or economic backgrounds?*
- *How might all students be encouraged to gain proficiency in more than one language? How can this accomplishment be measured and celebrated?*

Conflict Resolution

- *Learn more about how families from the cultural and identity groups the school serves manage conflict. Help staff, students, and community members understand that these cultural ways of being may lead to a misinterpretation of other people's intents in social interactions.*
- *Are there policies or practices on-site that marginalize certain groups of students or discriminate based on their demographic characteristics or background experiences?*
- *How are policies or practices upheld schoolwide and in each classroom to ensure that differences among students are valued, especially during conflict?*

at other grade levels and their families as well but found the "kindergarten approach" set a strong foundation for his work.

To feel included at school, students must sense that they are "known" there—that school staff and classmates see them as unique people who bring a range of background experiences, hopes, and ways of being. When people are known, their absence from school is noticed and missed. Chhuon and Wallace (2012) describe three "ways of knowing" students at school and how educators can move to develop these types of relationships: moving beyond "just teach" relationships, providing instrumental support, and giving students the benefit of the doubt. The first way of knowing involves looking beyond the curriculum to better understand the students for whom it is intended. This happens when educators move past seeing students solely as recipients of the learning material and listen and observe to better connect with the students. For example, an educator who engages students in conversations about their families' activities and learns about the students' interests is moving beyond "just teach" relationships. When students feel that their teachers understand their lives outside of school, they feel more "known" (Chhuon & Wallace, 2012).

A second way of helping students to feel known at school is for educators to provide instrumental support—dedicated teaching practices that aid students' individual success in focused ways (Chhuon & Wallace, 2012). For example, Kevin, a 5th grade Spanish and English bilingual student, received instrumental support from his teacher, who used many culturally sustaining practices, such as incorporating Spanish into classroom lessons, designing clear procedures and routines and using them coherently, and building what he knew was interesting to Kevin and some of his fellow students into presentations (Helman et al., 2016). Because Kevin heard his teacher valuing his home language and connecting the material to his music and sports interests, and he knew that he understood the classroom rules, procedures, and consequences, he felt that he belonged in the classroom and that his success was important to the teacher.

The third way to support students' feelings of being known at school, according to Chhuon and Wallace (2012), is for them to receive "benefit of the doubt" treatment there. This means that if something does not go well at school (e.g., homework is not finished, student is not following a rule), instead of categorizing students or their families negatively, educators hold the beliefs that students want to learn and be successful and that they care about others. Too often, students from marginalized groups feel under attack by the numerous forces of inequity they bump into every day in so many settings. If students feel unappreciated and misunderstood at school, they will doubt that educators see them as having value in the world and may disconnect from school-based activities and people. When this happens, students' strengths remain hidden and opportunities for connection at school are diminished. As an example of how "benefit of the doubt" treatment might take shape in a school setting, educators might ask students, "Tell me about what happened," or use empathy to elicit a response, such as "That must have been frustrating (scary, upsetting, etc.)", when something goes wrong.

In a longitudinal study of seven immigrant students as they moved from 1st through 6th grades, our research team discovered that several of the students attempted to stay under the radar at school (Helman et al., 2016). These students tried not to stand out or do anything wrong so as to be put in the spotlight. Unfortunately, this also meant that students were often judged by their behavior ("good") rather than becoming fully known academically and socially; and, in certain cases, students were not provided with the support needed to progress. This "hiding out" behavior can have serious consequences for student learning; school must become a place where students feel safe in showing what they know and don't know. Students who are learning English need to be able to try out their new language without being mimicked or stereotyped—when culturally or linguistically insensitive remarks are made, all school staff must address them forthrightly so that students feel safe and welcome. Chapter 5 addresses this topic through a linguistic lens.

Developing relationships at school is key for students' sense of belonging and inclusion in the learning community. Relationships of trust develop with opportunities to interact and learn about each other, openness to seeing what makes people unique and talented, and safe spaces for making mistakes and growing. Figure 4.2 presents three key sets of relationships that will help students feel connected to school: relationships with peers, relationships with school personnel, and the school's relationship with families.

FIGURE 4.2
A Variety of Relationships to Support Student Inclusion

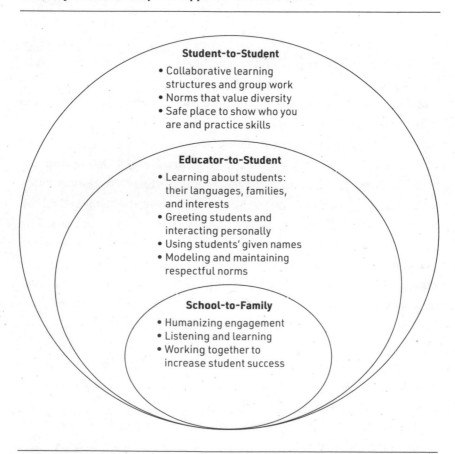

Student-to-Student
- Collaborative learning structures and group work
- Norms that value diversity
- Safe place to show who you are and practice skills

Educator-to-Student
- Learning about students: their languages, families, and interests
- Greeting students and interacting personally
- Using students' given names
- Modeling and maintaining respectful norms

School-to-Family
- Humanizing engagement
- Listening and learning
- Working together to increase student success

Chapter 2 explored how to form trusting connections with families and communities, a foundational relationship for students' success at school. The second circle of connection in Figure 4.2 highlights the ways educators can develop stronger relationships directly with their students. Although each educator is unique in style and personality—some may use curiosity or humility to build bonds while others may feature humor or storytelling—certain educator behaviors always help students feel connected. These include saying hello and good-bye, learning and using students' real names (not making up "easier to pronounce" versions), finding time to speak individually or in small groups, helping out when needed, learning about what is happening outside of class, mentoring, and maintaining safe spaces for students to express who they are and what they know. An observation guide highlighting aspects of the physical environment that support inclusion in included in the Appendix (Figure A.2).

The third circle of connection in Figure 4.2 draws attention to the important role that peers have in helping students feel included, or not, at school. Students will vary in the depths and numbers of friendships they have at school; however, all students should feel welcome and safe there. This means that educators and school leaders have responsibility for structuring the groundwork for, and ensuring the maintenance of, respectful behavior among students. This structure is aided by more opportunities to work together cooperatively and fewer occasions when students are pitted against one another. When students are guided in how to work in teams and are rewarded for their collective accomplishments, peer relationships grow and group identity blossoms. This means that not only should emergent bilinguals be included in collaborative group work in class or on schoolwide projects, but everyone also should be mentored in teamwork skills, such as how to communicate across languages, how to resolve disagreements, and what it looks like to solicit the input of team members.

One area of relationship building not called out in Figure 4.2 is the staff-to-staff relationship that a school leader is called upon to facilitate. Although this relationship does not include students directly, it has an impact when staff work together to create individual student success plans, analyze student performance data, or influence one another's mindsets—either positively or negatively—about students. Chapter 8 investigates how educational leaders can structure productive relationships among staff through professional learning communities that center around student success as a collaborative goal.

Taking the Next Step: From an Inclusive Climate to a Culture That Centers Equity

If climate is the feeling one gets when experiencing life in a school, its physical and social environments, and the way people relate to one another, then culture may be thought of as the unwritten guidelines, beliefs, and assumptions that exist in the organization that tend to steer all behavior toward *how we do it here* (Gruenert & Whitaker, 2015). Organizational culture is the way one generation passes down what it has learned to the next and is, in effect, a "collective programming of the mind" (Hofstede, 1997). As such, school culture is more difficult to uncover and makes changing what lies below the surface more difficult (Gruenert & Whitaker, 2015). Words such as *entrenched*, *unexamined*, *social reinforcement*, and the like highlight the potential need to take an inclusive setting one step further, moving from climate to a long-lasting culture based on principles of equity for marginalized students.

When innovative practices are introduced in a school, such as some of the ideas presented in this book, the efforts can have initially positive results. Nonetheless, when there are bumps in the road, the traditional site culture may subtly take control again, negating the progress that has been made. It is critical that deeper, more long-lasting work takes place that will have an impact on staff beliefs and empower students and their families to contribute to and oversee the school culture. Based on the efforts of schools that have had success in creating cultures of equity before, some related findings are noted here (Hanover Research, 2017; NAESP, n.d.; Wentworth, Kessler, & Darling-Hammond, 2013):

- *Leaders.* Developing a culture of equity requires dedicated and vision-focused principals who support teacher recruitment and development. Steady leadership is needed to embed change through modeling and facilitation.

- *Resources*. Schools make the most of existing resources and ensure that these are used to work toward equity goals and the inclusive vision. Schoolwide services are coordinated to address students' varying needs. Budgeting is conducted with the vision in mind.
- *Trust*. Schools develop relational trust among all members of the school community, including meaningful educator collaboration with family members.
- *Differentiation*. Schools use assessment data and educator professional learning time to create personalized instructional plans and conceptualize culturally responsive pedagogical approaches.
- *Learning about culture*. Staff reflect on their own dispositions toward various forms of diversity and unconscious bias, and they learn to teach in more culturally and linguistically responsive ways. This is likely to involve cultural self-assessment, teaching from a culturally inclusive perspective, monitoring discourse styles, and being sensitive to different forms of conflict resolution.
- *Involve students*. Educational leaders empower students through diversity leadership training so that they can train peers and advise educators on issues of inclusion, tolerance, and conflict resolution. Staff open up opportunities for students to set goals for their own learning and monitor their success in attaining their goals. Learning goals are centered around not only the content of academic standards but also skills that are transferable to work life, civic engagement, and personal relations, such as communicating, critiquing, questioning, collaborating, and analyzing.

Each school community can apply these research-based findings to their setting in ways that build on local strengths, challenges, and goals. For example, one school community that had improved their procedures for data collection to inform differentiated instruction felt that the way they presented data at conferences was not meaningful to family members. Staff studied the issue and found resources that helped them to adapt the format for these conversations (Garcia, Frunzi, Dean, Flores, & Miller, 2016). First, staff members practiced how to describe assessment data in terms understandable by noneducators. Next, a structure for the meetings was outlined that ensured the conversation would incorporate information from both home and school settings. To prepare even more fully for the interactions, staff practiced the data conversations with peers sitting in as family members. During these role-plays, they were able to try out skills such as presuming positive intent, paraphrasing, and asking powerful questions to support student achievement. As a final step in preparation, staff members reflected on the experience, noting what they learned about making data more understandable to families, how to better interact using their home languages, how to support two-way communication, and ways to establish trust (see Garcia et al., 2016, for a detailed description).

If a school culture is a "framework for solving problems" (Gruenert & Whitaker, 2015), the culture must be embraced and enacted by all stakeholders, including leaders, teachers and other staff, students, family members, visitors, and the larger community. The ideas described in this section help create the visible and invisible structure for ensuring that cultural and linguistic inclusiveness become *the way it is done here*—the beliefs that guide the vision for improvement.

Summary

This chapter focused on creating a schoolwide environment that demonstrates an appreciation for the cultural and linguistic diversity of its students and families. A welcoming and inclusive school climate encompasses the physical environment; the norms that people use in their social relationships at school; and the collaborative and trusting relationships that are developed among leaders, staff, students, families, and other community members. Key to creating an inclusive school is establishing a collaborative vision statement that centers around equity for marginalized students. Moving beyond creating an inclusive climate, it is critical that thoughtful and long-term actions are taken to establish a culture that becomes the anchor for responsive and inclusive practices on-site. This happens when there is consistent leadership on the vision, each stakeholder in the community holds ownership for the goals, and culturally responsive practices are explored and implemented at the individual and systemwide levels.

Resources for Further Learning

Learn from the research on equity and inclusiveness at the schoolwide level by exploring these resources from educators and researchers who have put the ideas into practice. The following sources present many exemplary practices and links to other online resources:

- **National Association of Elementary School Principals—The Principal's Guide to Building Culturally Responsive Schools.** This brief guide contains words of wisdom from educational leaders and researchers to guide the work of making schools more equitable and culturally responsive. Each section highlights recommendations for practice and a list of resources and tools for learning more. Visit https://www.naesp.org/sites/default/files/NAESP_Culturally_Responsive_Schools_Guide.pdf.
- **Hanover Research—Closing the Gap: Creating Equity in the Classroom.** This brief summary of the research includes clear and straightforward ways to improve cultural competency for educators. The document includes a helpful list of engagement, learning environment, and feedback strategies to support equity in the classroom. Visit https://www.hanoverresearch.com/wp-content/uploads/2017/06/Equity-in-Education_Research-Brief_FINAL.pdf.
- **ASCD's School Culture and Climate Resources.** Browse books, articles, videos, and other resources from ASCD to learn about how to lead improvement in school climate and culture. Visit http://www.ascd.org/professional-development/school-climate-and-culture-resources.aspx.

Learning Through
a New Language:
A Primer for Leaders

Language is at the center of human behavior and learning. Think of a situation you might find yourself in and simply try to imagine that setting without language—it seems impossible. Humans communicate with others using language. We plan what we will do next in our day using language in our heads. We constantly observe the world around us and attach labels and sentences to what we see. A person looks outside a window and thinks, "It's raining; the wind is blowing leaves off of the tree." Without conscious realization, language permeates almost everything in our lives.

Language also connects to peoples' emotional lives and identities. The term *mother tongue* does not carry a purely academic meaning. It highlights the idea that a first language is given to children by their families and invokes an emotional connection to the people and memories they are closest to. Because language is such an intrinsic part of how people view themselves, how they interpret the world, and with whom they identify, it can never be considered a purely academic topic. As noted in Chapters 2–4, inclusive schoolwide practices that value diversity and multilingualism are key to creating safe linguistic spaces for children to learn and express themselves. Acquiring a new language is both an academic pursuit and a journey that leads to enlarging understandings of those who possess different languages or variations of languages.

Your school may feel like a global village with your families representing dozens of home languages or more. Or you may have emergent bilingual students from one primary home language. The school staff may represent linguistic diversity as well, especially if you offer dual immersion programs or other linguistic enrichment. Each school site is unique, and national data on the multilingual capabilities of teaching staff are not available. Nonetheless, student populations overall clearly are much more multilingual than the educators serving them. Bridging this educator awareness gap and ensuring that staff know how to best instruct students who are learning through a new language is of paramount importance to fostering academic success at school.

This chapter will examine the role of language in academic learning and what makes learning in a new language unique. Throughout the chapter, how school language is acquired, how educators scaffold instructional language to help students access the curriculum, and what this scaffolded instruction looks like in various grade levels and academic contexts will be explored. The chapter also offers ideas for what to notice in classrooms to ensure that students receive equitable access to the curriculum. Finally, tips for supporting instructional practices that increase the success of emergent bilingual students will be reviewed.

The Importance of Language in Academic Learning

Language is both a tool used for new learning and the fuel that powers the learning process. For example, children use language to ask questions about what they don't understand or are curious about. Known words and phrases help children to extend the reach of their understanding and learn even more. As they use language to gain knowledge, children connect new learning to the concepts and labels they already possess. It is difficult to disentangle cognition and language because they are closely entwined, and cognition is often assessed through language. Clearly, identifying children's learning must involve understanding their language processing and cognition (Deák, 2014). Language and conceptual development are interdependent and mutually beneficial. For this reason, all educators should be well versed in the need to support language in academic settings.

Emergent bilinguals possess a vast warehouse of knowledge and experiences to call upon in their thinking and learning. Because their knowledge exists in a language that is often not accounted for at school, however, students may find roadblocks to their use of language instead of being able to use it as a tool or fuel. Emergent bilinguals who are presented with academic material at school that has not been specially designed for them will look into their knowledge warehouse and may have difficulty finding the relevant storage areas to place their new learning. This happens when educators don't help students make connections between their home and new languages and experiences and often leads to limited uptake and problems with retention. When educators find ways to help students connect what is learned at school to the concepts and language that students already possess—often in their home language—greater learning will take place. Examples of these practices will be examined in later sections of this chapter.

A Brief Overview of Second Language Development and Language Learning

Several foundational ideas relating to language development are likely to be helpful to plan effectively for instruction with emergent bilinguals. You may find the components of linguistic proficiency valuable for refreshing your knowledge base on these topics.

Learning to communicate in an oral language involves a variety of proficiencies. First are the reciprocal skills of listening and speaking. Listening is the receptive and speaking is the expressive side of communication. Language learners tend to take in language first and then later venture to express it on their own. Social or interpersonal language is that used between people, often face-to-face, to communicate with an immediate audience. Interpersonal communication tends to use high-frequency words and simpler sentences or phrases, and it is supported by nonverbal gestures. In contrast to interpersonal communication, academic language use involves sophisticated and technical vocabulary that is often decontextualized. Developing academic language skills is a necessity for success in school; students are expected to understand the procedural words teachers use in class as well as more complex sentence structures and increasingly specific and nuanced vocabulary. Figure 5.1 highlights characteristics of settings that make listening and speaking more or less difficult.

COMPONENTS OF LINGUISTIC PROFICIENCY

- *Phonology*. The sounds of a particular language. Sounds of a home language are acquired developmentally in a natural way. Acquiring sounds in additional languages can be more challenging if they do not exist in the home language.

- *Semantics*. The meanings of words. Words in a first language are learned from the beginning of social interaction and correspond with conceptual development (labeling of new ideas). In a new language, speakers either connect the meaning of a word to one in their home language or learn the new word and concept for the first time.

- *Syntax*. The way sentences and phrases are constructed in a language involving, for example, the order of subjects, verbs, and objects. The syntax of a first language feels natural to the speaker. In an additional language, differences in syntactical rules may be challenging to a new speaker (e.g., the order of words in phrases such as *blue book* versus *libro azul* in Spanish [which translates literally as "book blue"]).

- *Morphology*. Constructing words with meaningful parts such as *pre+dic+tion = prediction*. In a first language, patterns of word creation are generally acquired without explicit instruction, such as for the conjugation of verbs (e.g., *play, plays, played*). In a new language, differences in verb conjugation and affixation need to be examined and learned.

- *Pragmatics*. The ways language is used in various settings. Pragmatics includes nonverbal components, such as gesturing, interpersonal spacing, appropriate eye contact, and the ways interlocutors speak in relation to their age or status in the community. Cultural norms influence pragmatic aspects of language use, and these are likely to vary across languages.

FIGURE 5.1

Listening and Speaking Made Easier or Harder

Less difficult > > > > > > > More difficult		
Face-to-face interaction Interaction with real-time cues to support pacing Understanding supported by objects, pointing, hand gestures, and other nonverbal cues Simpler language structures and familiar vocabulary Focus on communication, not linguistic correctness	Not face-to-face Interaction in a larger group Fewer opportunities for nonverbal cues Quicker flow of language Longer sentences Less-common vocabulary	Verbal input only Fast pace of speech Topic decontextualized from current location Complex language structures and discourse connectors Vocabulary highly specialized and rarely used outside of academic settings Pressure to perform in a linguistically correct manner

To apply the information in Figure 5.1 to a real educational setting, consider the following situation: A student who approaches a teacher to ask a question about a work assignment will experience much more linguistic support than will a student who hears that information presented quickly in a large group without nonverbal cues. Face-to-face, the teacher will observe whether the student understands and use nonverbal cues or a slower pace if needed.

Time for Proficiency to Develop

The time it takes to acquire a new language varies and depends on a number of factors, including the age and previous linguistic experiences of the learner, opportunities for focused instruction and practice in the new language, how closely related the new language is to known languages, the motivation for learning, and more (Helman et al., in press). Students learning a new language at school may attain a level of interpersonal proficiency within one to three years (Cummins, 1979). In contrast, proficiency in academic English may take four to seven years or more (Hakuta, Butler, & Witt, 2000). In each year of schooling, new academic language expectations arise, which means that, for students, the standards goalpost continues to move farther away.

Students generally progress from learning immediate survival language to receptive interpersonal language to becoming more expressive using high-frequency words in highly contextualized settings. Academic language—such as that needed to listen to lectures and complex procedural directions—will develop incrementally and require systematic cultivation, including connecting academic language to concepts and words students already know in a home language. In a longitudinal study of seven emergent bilinguals from 1st through 6th grades, the students' academic achievement varied widely, but all of the participants were challenged most by the acquisition of academic language in English (Helman et al., 2016).

Providing Learning Scaffolds for Emergent Bilinguals

Researchers have identified and recommended a number of instructional practices that support the linguistic accessibility of classroom material for emergent bilinguals (Baker et al., 2014; Goldenberg, 2013; Helman, 2016; Shanahan & Beck, 2006; Shatz & Wilkinson, 2010). Legislation in your state may require licensed teachers to take classes in specially designed academic instruction for language learners, or you may have purchased curriculum designed to guide your staff to make accommodations for students learning English. These best-practice strategies are important but can turn into a laundry list implemented in a rote manner and make the lesson-planning process cumbersome. In my work as a teacher and researcher, I've found that it helps to think about what makes a lesson linguistically difficult and then have a toolkit to build scaffolds for student access to the material. In the next several sections, how educators can teach more explicitly and systematically, connect their content to what students already know, find ways to increase student engagement, and build a mutually supportive learning community will be explored.

Use systematic and explicit instruction. Students learn best when the material is at their level of instructional need, it is presented in a clear and understandable way, and they have opportunities to practice their learning with the guidance of a knowledgeable instructor (Hattie,

2009; Helman, 2016). The following principles are helpful in carrying out this type of instruction:

- *Match instruction to students' levels of need.* Educators use formative assessments to learn about students' development along a continuum of learning (e.g., content standards or learning trajectory maps) within a particular subject matter (e.g., reading, word knowledge, mathematics). Flexible groupings are created to deliver "just right" instruction to meet students where they are and take them forward on the learning pathway for that specific area. For emergent bilinguals, matching instruction to students' levels of need also means understanding their language development in English so that material can be presented at their listening comprehension level.
- *Present content in multimodal and layered ways so that it is clear and understandable.* A number of strategies can be used to make content more comprehensible, including the use of photographs, drawings, charts, icons, and real objects (realia). Instructors can create written artifacts to augment their verbal directions, such as steps for carrying out an activity, lists of needed supplies, or procedure charts for how to participate in regular classroom routines. Modeling for students, showing a video of someone doing the activity, or analyzing an artifact of the task are additional ways to clearly demonstrate what students are expected to do. When the material is complex or multilayered, it is often helpful to cluster it into related sections. For example, instead of covering every aspect of bird life from the start of a unit, students may find that learning about the unique topics of nesting, feeding, habitat, and migration in smaller units may be easier to absorb. Explicitness can also be called upon by moving from simple cases to more complex ones. For example, compound words are a simple way to begin to discuss morphology (e.g., *sun* + *shine* = *sunshine*) that can lead to an examination of words that are much more complex (e.g., *man* + *u* + *fac* + *ture* = *manufacture*).

Language-focused scaffolds can also make the content clearer and more understandable. Metacognition, the process of talking through an activity or "thinking out loud," is a way to help students understand the content of the lesson or the expectations for their work in class. Instructors can use students' home languages to connect in-class content to what they already know or to clarify misconceptions. For students to understand content, they need to know the meanings of 90 percent of the words presented in the lesson. In particular, key conceptual or procedural vocabulary that is unknown will need to be explicitly identified and taught. Later in this chapter, vignettes of what this vocabulary-embedded instruction might look like in various settings are explored.

The level of systematic and explicit instruction needed will vary depending on the students being taught. For this reason, it is never enough for an educator to think, "I explained that so clearly and demonstrated it well!" Throughout the lesson, educators must consistently check for understanding of the material by eliciting questions from students, asking them to demonstrate a concept on paper or using their bodies, or having them restate key ideas to a partner. Only if student understanding has been demonstrated will educators know that they have been systematic and explicit enough in their instruction.

• *Provide opportunities for guided practice.* An important aspect of systematic and explicit instruction is for learners to try out the activity and get feedback on their performance (Hattie & Yates, 2014). The space where this practice happens with the assistance of a knowledgeable other is often referred to as the zone of proximal development (Vygotsky, 1978). Practice within one's ZPD—being able to try out learning that one can't yet do independently—is necessary to gain skills in almost everything, from reading a challenging text, to conducting a science experiment, to operating a complex machine. Educators structure guided practice in a number of ways: They organize small-group instruction so that they can observe and "coach" students in the new practice; they structure partner work within the class or by finding partners from "buddy" classes to help; and they use resource people, such as classroom volunteers, university practicum students, specialist teachers, or members of the community. Moving forward, adaptive computer-based programs may also become more ubiquitous in providing guided practice support for students in a variety of fields.

Connect to what students know. Learning theory highlights that new knowledge attaches to previous understandings that are related (Anderson & Pearson, 2002). Exploring students' personal experiences and background knowledge is a key first step that effective educators take as they plan and implement their curriculum. Emergent bilinguals often possess background experiences that could help them understand academic content in class; however, these experiences may go unnoticed because of the communication gap with their teachers across languages. Therefore, it is incumbent on educators to find ways to learn about the knowledge and experiences that students bring to class and use scaffolded instruction to help learners connect what they know to the new content. To find out more about what students already know, educators can do the following:

- Conduct informal assessments of students' multilingual skills, including what languages they speak, read, and write. If necessary, find school personnel or community members who speak students' home languages to help analyze their literacy strengths. When doing preassessments in class, invite students to show what they know in their home language.
- Invite students to share personal histories through both writing and drawing or other media; this can inform lesson planning.
- Survey students or their parents about background experiences, including places they have lived, responsibilities they have taken on, skills they have, or what they are most interested in.
- With each new unit of study, invite students to share what they already know about the topic and what they would like to learn. Find ways for all students to show what they know, even if they are not yet fluent writers in English.

- Use anticipation guides (Herber, 1978) to have students show their background knowledge about a topic coming up in the classroom. For example, an anticipation guide could ask students to decide if a set of statements is true or false, if they agree or disagree with a proposition, or if they can identify an object within a set that doesn't belong (Helman, Cramer, Johnston, & Bear, 2017). How students respond to the prompts will help educators learn about their background knowledge and tailor the upcoming unit more appropriately.

Once information has been gathered about students' background experiences in relation to the upcoming content, educators can intentionally build bridges between what students know and what they will learn in class. The following ideas are only a beginning set of the many ways this might be done:

- Use graphic organizers to highlight connections between previous knowledge and new learning. For example, have students create a concept map with what they already know about a topic, and then use a different color to add what they learn in class.
- Keep reflection journals and use prompts such as, "I used to think _____, but now I know _____."
- Have students keep track of the ways their home languages and English are similar or different. This may be done in a personal notebook or collectively on chart paper in the class.
- Encourage students to use all of their linguistic knowledge, including languages other than English, when composing essays or creating class projects. Multilingual projects allow students to express themselves more completely, and translations can always be added later for anyone who does not speak one of the languages.
- Tell stories that make the content being studied more tangible. For example, a story that students can identify with involving the need for measurement might be a good "hook" at the beginning of a mathematics unit.
- Have students use sticky notes in their textbooks or reading materials to make connections to their background experiences.

- When a new area of study is introduced that students have limited background experiences with, follow a whole-to-part-to-whole sequence for presenting it. First, show what the area involves in the real world (whole); then, show what components are involved within the topic or process (part); and, finally, reconnect with how the new learning takes shape in students' lives (whole). For example, when beginning a unit on fractions, a teacher could begin with a real-life example of a need to divide something into pieces, such as a pan of brownies. How many people will be coming to the party? How many ways could the rectangular-shaped pan be divided so that each person gets as large a piece as possible?

Finding out what students already know (their networks of schemata) and scaffolding instruction to connect new learning to this knowledge base helps students do more schema building and thereby enlarge their storehouse of conceptual understandings.

Facilitate student engagement. Active engagement with content is more likely to result in long-term learning, and this is especially true for students experiencing schooling in a new language (Philp & Duchesne, 2016). Instead of simply listening to material presented by a teacher, deeper learning takes place when a student puts the learning into practice through a purposeful activity or through a project that is important in the real world or allows them to interact with others in meaningful ways. The Appendix includes an observation guide (Figure A.5) with ideas for what to look for and collect date on regarding students' engagement and learning.

Engagement is enhanced in different ways for students. Some students will be motivated by creative art projects, poetry, or music. Others will appreciate time to talk about the academic topic with others in a small-group setting. Everyone is more engaged when there is choice in what they study or how they demonstrate their learning. The following suggestions are a first step for how student engagement can be used to scaffold learning for emergent bilinguals:

- *Monitor teacher talk time in class*. During instruction, insert frequent opportunities for students to participate, such as through partner shares, physical activity, or self-reflection.
- *Structure various ways for students to show what they know*, such as through drawing, writing in their home language, in small groups or partnerships, by building something, or through drama or music.
- *Provide choice* whenever possible.
- *Find out what motivates students* and incorporate examples that reflect their interests in course content as a "hook."
- *Be aware of how much sitting and listening students are required to do*. This is not the most effective way for emergent bilingual students to learn, and they will likely reach linguistic overload if they don't have a chance to think through, discuss, ask questions about, or put into practice the material at regular intervals.

Build a learning community. Students who are held to high expectations and given support to reach these academic goals are much more likely to be successful at school (Boser, Wilhelm, & Hanna, 2014; Hakuta, 2018). This means that emergent bilingual students must feel they are important members of the classroom community and are valued for who they are and what they bring to class. Emergent bilinguals should not be separated into a certain section of the classroom or always find themselves interacting only with other emergent bilinguals. Here are some ways to make all students feel included:

- *Set and maintain norms for classroom interactions that uphold respect for all and do not tolerate put-downs*. If students are belittled about their English language skills or other identity markers, they will come to see classroom norms as only a façade and could become intimidated about expressing themselves.
- *Provide many opportunities for students to work with diverse peers in collaborative groups in a variety of ways*.
- *Find multiple ways to value cultural, linguistic, economic, religious, gender, and ability-based diversity within the classroom community*. This acceptance can be demonstrated through posters in the

classroom, the inclusion of culturally and linguistically diverse books and materials, interest in languages other than English, and discussions that make a safe space for students to express who they are and where they come from without being categorized as unusual or deficient (e.g., different language, different religion, different clothing or food preferences, different access to financial resources).

- *Create a low-anxiety environment in which students feel comfortable asking questions and trying out a new language without fear of being ridiculed.* To learn a new language, a lot of practice is needed. Asking questions is a sign of interest and learning, not a deficiency. If students are afraid of being laughed at or mimicked, they will likely keep quiet and will be robbed of opportunities to become more proficient in their language skills. Conscientious educators will encourage students to share their confusions so that they can be clarified. Learning communities are places where empathy for others is nurtured, and peers help one another so that all can succeed. Posted norms, consistent monitoring and reinforcement by teachers and peers, and frequent classroom discussions about what a "mistake-making place" looks, sounds, and feels like are crucial to maintaining a safe learning environment.

What This Looks Like in Practice

As noted earlier in this chapter, a key component of systematic and explicit instruction is to ensure that students understand the meanings of the words presented in class. For emergent bilinguals who are unlikely to know all of the language in the material they hear and read in class, every lesson is a language-learning opportunity. Some suggestions presented so far in this chapter include the use of visuals and realia, looking for content that is at students' listening comprehension levels, providing demonstrations, thinking out loud, and presenting the content in culturally familiar ways. This section takes a look into three classroom moments that involve language that may be unfamiliar to students and consider the educator's use of vocabulary-embedded instruction.

Vocabulary-Embedded Instruction in a 1st Grade Language Arts Lesson

Ms. R begins the reading workshop in her classroom by bringing students together on the rug for an introduction to the day's goals and activities. Expectations for the day are written on the whiteboard, and each item on the list is illustrated with a small icon. For example, "buddy reading" is illustrated with a drawing of two children sitting side-by-side with books in their laps. Today the class is focused on asking questions about their reading, so Ms. R has selected some key words to reinforce for students: *question, ask, answer, details,* and *character.* These words are printed on index cards and, as each word is presented, Ms. R invites two students to act out the word's meaning. She uses a page from a recent big book she read to the whole class to serve as a prop for the vocabulary explanations. For example, when acting out what the word *character* means, the students refer to the young protagonist of the big book. Following this introduction, students meet with their reading buddies and practice asking and answering questions about details in their own independent reading books and finding out about the characters in each other's books.

In the quick minilesson just described, Ms. R has introduced key vocabulary related to the class's learning targets; involved students in highly engaging physical and social activity; provided written guides to support them; and set them up for independent, collaborative work in which they will use the new language in context.

Vocabulary-Embedded Instruction in a 4th Grade Mathematics Lesson

Mr. H is in week two of a unit on quadrilaterals, but he has noticed that his students continue to confuse the concepts of *parallel* and *intersecting lines.* He has shown his students several images of what these terms mean, but the awareness has yet to take hold. He has three new ideas for what to do at the beginning of week two. First, he plans to use students' home languages to define the key words. Many of the students speak Spanish at home, and he has discovered that these two words reflect cognates in Spanish—*parallel* is *paralelo* in Spanish and *intersection* is *intersección*. Mr. H has two students who speak Vietnamese at home, and he knows that it contains few cognates with English. Nonetheless, he intends to use an online translation site to have students look up the meanings of these words and use the translations as they participate. Next, Mr. H will invite students in partnerships to discuss a series of objects that he presents, such as a clock, a chess board, and a road map. In their home language or English, the partners will decide if the objects contain parallel or intersecting lines. When the partners have decided together, they will call out the agreed-upon term in English or Spanish or Vietnamese. A final step for cementing this vocabulary for future work will be for students to work with a partner to identify five things in the classroom or school that contain parallel or intersecting lines. Each partnership will submit labeled drawings highlighting where in the object various types of lines are present.

In this lesson plan, Mr. H has used the strategies of partner learning, calling on the home language, and multimodal experiences. He has moved through several steps of explicit instruction, including demonstrating, guided practice, and independent work.

Vocabulary-Embedded Instruction in a 7th Grade Science Lesson

Ms. T is working with students on a unit related to climate events and changes in the Earth's environment. She has reviewed the textbook chapter and identified 10 key words or phrases that are critical for students to understand as they tackle the information: *climate, weather, pollution, ozone layer, ultraviolet rays, absorption, evaporation, precipitation, greenhouse effect,* and *glaciers.* Ms. T begins her lesson with an anticipation guide, asking students a set of true or false statements relating to their understanding of the key words. Next, she asks students to find a partner and review their answers to see if they are the same or different. When they are finished with their review and discussion, she opens the floor to questions from the students about what is still confusing to them. She has selected a set of digital photographs that illustrate each term and uses these to supplement her responses to students' questions. Next, Ms. T invites students to break into groups with three members based on their interest in how to illustrate the words. Groups can draw what the terms represent; look up the etymology of the words and make connections to other known words; act out the terms; create a poem, rhyme, or chant; or create questions for a quiz related to the meanings of the words to give to their peers. The following day in class, students will present their products to fellow students.

In this lesson, Ms. T has thoughtfully identified the most important vocabulary her students will need to acquire, supported their engagement in fun and social ways, given students a choice for how to demonstrate their learning of the vocabulary, and provided multiple opportunities for review and reinforcement of the word meanings.

What to Look for in a Language-Learning Classroom

Each classroom is unique because of its collection of students with various backgrounds and interests working along with the strengths of the teacher and other educators who contribute to the learning community. Within these diverse contexts, common teaching practices and environmental supports can be identified through which emergent bilinguals receive the highest level of support for learning English and putting it to use. In the sections that follow, sample practices are outlined for the physical environment, educator actions, and student behaviors.

The Physical Environment

In a language-learning classroom, the physical space in the room serves as a guide and a resource for student learning. A brief scan of the room communicates what the class is studying and where students might go to find help. Walking into a language-rich classroom, a visitor might see the following:

- Charts outlining various classroom procedures that are clearly written and illustrated with visuals
- A daily agenda illustrated with visuals
- Class norms with illustrations that demonstrate that the space is safe for mistake making and that community members help one another to succeed
- Picture cards with key vocabulary for current units of study, along with labels in English and potentially the home languages of students
- English labels for classroom materials illustrated with visuals
- Books, posters, study aids, and other materials in English and students' home languages
- Desks and tables organized so that students are able to meet and work in groups
- Space for the teacher to meet with small groups of students for differentiated lessons
- Notes or lists on chart paper to help students expand their English writing capabilities (e.g., "Other words to use instead of *said*" or "Conjunctions used for making longer sentences").

An observation guide highlighting key things to look for in the physical environment is included in the Appendix (Figure A.3).

Educator Actions

The teacher and other educators in the classroom serve as leaders to uphold community norms and maintain the safety of all students' participation. As such, a visitor notices that if the class norms are broken, the educators address this behavior directly in a sensitive way, rather than letting it slide. Educators are well prepared with support materials, including visuals. They use language that is understandable to students, introduce and clarify new vocabulary or complex language structures, speak clearly and directly to students, and regularly check for understanding.

Educators scaffold language learning by meeting with groups of emergent bilinguals to preview or review content vocabulary from group lessons and find out whether students have background experiences relating to this content. As a regular part of each lesson, educators embed time for students to practice using the content language with guidance—perhaps through the use of sentence frames—or in conversation with peers. Teachers and specialists work collaboratively to plan activities that consistently advance the academic English of emergent bilingual students. The observation guide in the Appendix (Figure A.4) highlights a number of educator actions that support language development in the classroom.

Student Behaviors

First and foremost, when walking into a language-learning classroom the visitor notices that students are actively engaged. Often, students are interacting with others discussing a topic or working collaboratively on a project. Students know where to find learning support materials, such as bilingual dictionaries. When participating in an educator-guided lesson, students are responsible for being involved in some way—taking notes, responding with physical cues, or periodically sharing with partners.

In a language-learning classroom, students ask questions when they are confused and help one another when someone gets stuck. One can hear the use of languages other than English as students share their ideas and ask for clarification. Students are willing to try out unknown English vocabulary and syntax because they know it will help them get better at the language. Students have ways to document their learning, such as in personal notebooks, individual word walls, bilingual dictionaries, and other personalized reference materials. The observation guide in the Appendix (Figure A.4) highlights a number of student behaviors that are likely to be evident in a language-learning classroom.

Tips for Strengthening Teaching Behaviors That Support Language Learning

How can a school leader encourage the teaching behaviors outlined in this chapter? Educators often think that when a leader enters the classroom, he expects to hear silence. But silence is not where good language learning happens. Here are some first steps for encouraging educators to become more intentional facilitators of language learning:

- Let educators know that emergent bilingual students need many opportunities to practice English. Share your expectations that classroom spaces should reflect student learning through language.
- Use staff meeting time to share approaches to vocabulary instruction. The first five minutes of every meeting could highlight one example of how an educator embedded vocabulary in a unit of study.
- Provide resources to be used for visuals and realia. For example, find ways for educators to share digital photo resources, boxes of picture cards, or real-life objects related to their common areas of study.
- As noted in Chapter 4, set up schoolwide expectations that encourage students to cooperate and support one another and make sure that their classroom learning environment follows these guidelines so that students feel safe trying out their burgeoning language skills.
- Create a safe environment for teachers to try out new strategies and ask questions. Encourage partner or grade-level teams to collaboratively set goals and support one another's learning.
- Use professional learning time to examine artifacts of student work and share successful teaching practices. For example, student writing can be analyzed to better understand their language development. Then, once academic language needs have been identified, colleagues can test out ways to support language learning to find out what has the greatest impact on their students.
- Share the observation guides in the Appendix that focus on teacher behaviors that support a language-learning classroom, ways to create physical spaces for language learning, and how to gather data on student engagement. Use the forms to provide regular feedback to teachers on what is working and what could be enhanced to support language learning in the classroom.

Summary

This chapter focused on the crucial role of language in academic learning and how important it is for educators and educational leaders to understand the contexts that support language development. Learning in a new language requires specially designed teaching—from providing clear and explicit instruction, to using multimodal learning strategies, to calling on the learner's previous knowledge. This learning happens best when students experience a low-anxiety environment in which they are able to practice their new language skills in a supportive community. Several examples of vocabulary-embedded instruction that used scaffolded instructional techniques at various grade levels were explored. The chapter concluded with a list of observable behaviors and environmental artifacts that might be evidence of a classroom that supports language learning and a few ideas for how educational leaders might encourage their staffs to support language development more intentionally.

Resources for Further Learning

The following websites provide information about language development in the classroom. Each link will lead you to a wealth of resources:

- **Your State's English Language Development (ELD) Standards and Resources.** Each state follows a set of developmental goals based on their ELD assessments and standards. The agencies connected to these standards have numerous resources and a developmental continuum to call upon. See, for example:
  - WIDA: Used by 39 states and territories. Visit https://wida.wisc.edu/.
  - California English language development standards. Visit https://www.cde.ca.gov/sp/el/er/eldstandards.asp.
  - New York State English as a Second Language. Visit http://www.p12.nysed.gov/assessment/nyseslat/.

— Supporting English learners in Texas. Visit http://www.elltx. org/index.html.

- **What Works Clearinghouse—Teaching Academic Content and Literacy to English Learners in Elementary and Middle School.** This summary of the evidence base on instruction with English learners is available as a downloaded Educator's Practice Guide. Visit http://ies.ed.gov/ncee/wwc/Docs/practiceguide/ english_learners_pg_040114.pdf.

- **Center for Applied Linguistics.** This nonprofit organization is dedicated to sharing information about how to support teaching and learning for culturally and linguistically diverse people. Its website houses numerous research articles about language learning and links to other organizations, including the Sheltered Instruction Observation Protocol. Visit http://www.cal.org/.

Evidence-Based Practices in the Literacy Classroom

Instructional leaders have many responsibilities in their work, from leading school goal setting and collaborative planning, to supervising staff, to creating structures for parent and community interaction, and much more. Although some instructional leaders have strong foundational knowledge in reading and writing development, perhaps by having been primary-grade teachers responsible for literacy instruction in the past, many others bring different background experiences to their leadership positions. Whether or not you personally bring a depth of pedagogical knowledge about literacy learning and teaching, it is critical that, as an elementary or middle school leader, you must be confident that the teaching practices occurring on-site are based on research that shows their effectiveness for all students (Helman & Pekel, in press). Leaders also need to have a general understanding of how literacy instruction varies depending on students' ages and capabilities in reading and writing. Leaders have responsibilities for structuring opportunities for their staff to meet regularly to examine student progress, share the most recent knowledge base on literacy learning and instruction, and build capacity among staff to understand and address students' literacy learning needs (ILA, 2018).

This chapter covers foundational principles that are essential for powerful literacy instruction to take place in elementary and middle school classrooms. For each key idea presented, examples are provided that will help you envision what would be taking place in classrooms of various grade levels should this principle be firmly in place. This chapter highlights instruction that would typically occur in class periods identified as *reading, writing, language arts, reading intervention,* or *reader's and writer's workshop*. The use of evidence-based language and literacy practices in content-area classrooms, including *English* or *literature*, will be highlighted in Chapter 7.

Literacy Learning Is a Developmental Process

Readers and writers develop in predictable and observable ways. Some students may learn to read quickly and seemingly as if by magic, and others may take time and much effort with the process. Still, the basic steps everyone goes through to become capable readers follow parallel paths. During a period of *emergent literacy*, a person begins to differentiate between text and other visuals and develops an awareness of the cadence of language in various written forms. Depending on exposure to written materials, emergent readers begin to memorize simple chunks of text—such as rhymes, names, or other important information—and mimic the reading of others. Over time, emergent readers become more accurate in identifying letters as distinct from numbers or shapes that resemble letters. In alphabetic languages such as English, emergent readers learn the names of the letters and begin to attach a sound to each letter. This guides the learner to the realization that writing is not simply a series of random strings of letters but, instead, represents an alphabetic principle. An awareness that letters represent sounds in predictable ways is the beginning step toward "breaking the code" of English—a huge step on the literacy journey.

Beginning readers consolidate their understanding of sound-symbol relationships, or phonics, in the English writing system step-by-step, by sound and letter. Beginning readers are testing out their newly acquired skills first by applying what they know about phonics in very simple materials that also have words they have memorized by sight. Readers at this level will initially be slow and labored in their reading, and they may have difficulty holding together the meaning of longer sentences. Over time, beginning readers become more proficient by getting lots of practice reading materials that are not too difficult for them. Much like a person going to the gym, beginning readers become stronger and more capable by reading increasingly difficult texts that help them to use their new muscles without overwhelming them.

Transitional readers have become automatic in reading many of the words contained in primary-grade texts and show increasing fluency in their reading. At this level, students prefer silent reading because it allows them to read more quickly, and they work to become more proficient with decoding longer, multisyllable words. Transitional readers seek out simple chapter books and often get "hooked" on books that come in a series, whether mysteries, informational texts, or character-driven fiction. As students use their reading and writing skills, they increase in their ability to access more and more books in the elementary school library or children's section of the public library. Helping students develop a passion for reading is one way to nudge them forward to the intermediate and advanced levels of reading that will support their success at the upper elementary and secondary grade levels.

Intermediate readers might typically be described as reading at the upper elementary and middle school levels. They can access longer chapter books with hundreds of pages, although typically these texts are not as dense as material designed for adults. When students have particular interests and background knowledge, they are often able to read material with specialized vocabulary in that field. Students, in a manner similar to adult readers, develop preferences and niches for their reading habits. As they continue to read and write in a variety of genres and content areas, students grow to become *advanced readers*, reading fiction and informational texts on a range of topics in longer and more complex texts. The vocabulary and language structures in these texts are likely to be dense, and advanced readers who read deeply within a topic or genre are likely to read faster and with greater comprehension in that area.

It is important for instructional leaders to have foundational knowledge of how readers develop because appropriate instruction looks different for readers at different points in their development. Students within individual classrooms are likely to be at different levels of reading proficiency, and the instruction they receive and types of practice they engage in will need to be appropriate to their needs as advancing readers. It is important for educators and instructional leaders to share common vocabulary about literacy development and how various groups of students are progressing. It is also important for leaders to note that students in a single classroom will be at multiple developmental levels (Helman, 2016). For this reason, differentiation should be structured so that all students can receive literacy instruction at a level of "just-right" challenge. If a skills-based literacy lesson is delivered to the whole class, the lesson is likely to be developmentally appropriate for only some of the students, not all of them.

Emergent bilinguals develop literacy proficiency through the same progression. Understanding their development can be more complex for educators, however, and throughout this chapter, how instruction is tailored for students learning a new language while simultaneously learning to read and write in that language is explored. For example, students may bring literacy from another home language to their monolingual English classroom setting. In such a case, students should not be considered emergent readers; rather, they need help transferring their literacy abilities to the new language. In other cases, students may develop proficiency in decoding written English but may be stymied by a constrained language repertoire in their new language. These students need opportunities to learn the vocabulary in their texts at the same time they learn to break the code. These and other examples related to teaching emergent bilinguals are discussed in this chapter.

Literacy Learning Combines Foundational Skills with Language Knowledge

The act of reading requires two significant capabilities: the abilities to decode written text and then to extract the meaning that it holds. Neither of these activities alone suffices for "real reading" to occur. Scarborough (2001) has described the strands that weave together to form a strong cord of increasingly strategic and skilled reading: language comprehension and word recognition. Language comprehension includes the words and language structures that students know and use, as well as how students use their background knowledge, reasoning skills, and awareness of print and literate forms. Word recognition involves applying spelling sounds and patterns to the decoding of written words (Scarborough, 2001). Even in the simplest view of the reading process, researchers note that it takes both decoding and language-based skills for a reader to be proficient (Gough & Tunmer, 1986; Lesaux & Marietta, 2011). Figure 6.1 captures these two essential elements working together for proficient reading.

FIGURE 6.1
Language and Decoding Work to Support Skilled Reading

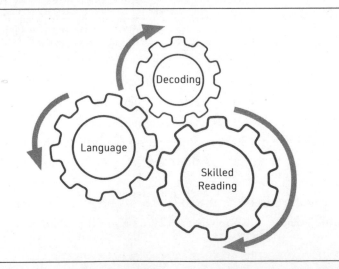

The National Reading Panel outlined five key elements of reading in their research review (NICHD, 2000), and they include both the code-related and language-based proficiencies that educators need to build on to help students become capable readers. The areas the panel highlighted were language/vocabulary, phonemic awareness, phonics, fluency, and comprehension. Figure 6.2 defines these core literacy components and describes their relationship to literacy development and instruction.

Figure 6.2 reinforces how language and foundational skills work together to support capable reading. If students do not know the meanings of words or cannot disentangle complex language structures, they will not be able to comprehend. Furthermore, knowing more words in a language supports being able to isolate specific sounds (phonemic awareness). Accurately decoding words using phonics is key to developing fluent reading. Skills and meaning are partners in proficient reading, and—especially for emergent bilinguals—the language knowledge embedded in an academic task should never be overlooked.

Informal literacy assessments should be in common use and frequently discussed among grade-level teams of educators. These literacy assessments will highlight where along the continuum of acquisition students are with each of the core literacy components. Informal assessments also help teachers identify students who need additional support to meet grade-level benchmarks in literacy. Consider the following examples of formative assessments that might be readily visible during visits to classrooms or under discussion in grade-level team meetings:

- *Language/vocabulary*. Students complete graphic organizers defining important words and phrases or self-assess their knowledge of vocabulary words.
- *Phonemic awareness*. Students orally produce rhyming words, words that begin with the same sound as ____, or words formed by blending a series of sounds (e.g., /b/+/i/+/g/ makes *big*).
- *Phonics*. Students identify the sounds represented by letters or groups of letters on a printed page, decode phonetically regular words in their texts, or show their phonics knowledge through developmental spelling samples.

FIGURE 6.2
Core Literacy Components

Core Component	What It Is	Developmental Connection
Language/ vocabulary	Knowledge of the meaning of words, phrases, and concepts as well as the syntactic structures to use them in reading, writing, speaking, and listening.	Unless language/vocabulary is in place for a particular academic task, reading and writing will lack meaning and will be a disconnected and rote task. Language/ vocabulary is the foundation for comprehension.
Phonemic awareness	The awareness that oral language can be broken into individual sounds that do not express meaning in themselves. For example, the word *sun* can be broken into the sounds (phonemes) /s/+/u/+/n/.	Phonemic awareness is a foundational skill on which an understanding of sound-symbol relationships may be built. Until students can isolate individual sounds in words, instruction in phonics will not be productive.
Phonics	The study of sound-symbol relationships such as letter sounds, vowel patterns, and multisyllable word decoding.	Phonics holds the key to decoding words in any alphabetic language. As students become more accurate and automatic in applying sound-symbol relationships during reading, they gain fluency, allowing them to more easily comprehend the material.
Fluency	The ability to read with sufficient rate and expression so that meaning can be held together.	Fluency flows from the accurate and automatic application of phonics. Fluency develops from frequent opportunities to read. Being a fluent reader makes it much easier to comprehend what is being read.
Comprehension	Understanding, extracting meaning from, and/or making connections to what is read.	Comprehension is the goal of reading and is highly dependent on the integration of the core literacy components. It is also related to the background knowledge and language/vocabulary that students possess. Working with emergent and beginning readers, educators can support comprehension by reading aloud and discussing more complex texts than students can access on their own.

- *Fluency.* Students read aloud texts at their instructional and independent levels while the teacher monitors rate and expression and documents growth in number of words and smoothness in one-minute readings.
- *Comprehension.* Students respond orally or in writing to comprehension questions about their reading materials, or they retell stories or information from texts.

Artifacts from informal assessments are important data for teachers to examine in their collaborative meetings. If students are identified who need additional support, this may take the form of small-group focused instruction in class or tiered intervention (as described in Chapter 3).

Developing Readers Need Explicit Instruction in the Core Elements

Unlike learning to speak in one's mother tongue, learning to read requires focused instruction in the core elements of language/vocabulary, phonemic awareness, phonics, fluency, and comprehension. For students learning in a new language, explicit instruction is even more critical. It is for this reason that publishers create teacher's manuals and lesson plans designed to show how to structure literacy instruction, often including accommodations for language learners. More important than any teacher guide, however, is an educator's knowledge of how to embed the core literacy elements into learning activities at their grade level based on students' development and language levels. To ensure that important evidence-based practices and learning opportunities are taking place in their schools, instructional leaders need foundational knowledge relating to the core literacy components and what they look like in practice.

Although literacy instruction varies across grade levels in K–8 classrooms, common principles and structures should be evident in all settings. When visiting a classroom or taking stock of a teacher's reading or writing lesson, instructional leaders should be able to see a focus on one or more of the core literacy components. For example, in a kindergarten or 1st grade classroom, there should be evidence that students are explicitly learning about the sounds of English and how they map to print in systematic ways (phonemic awareness and phonics). A visitor should see reading and writing centers with alphabet strips or sound-picture cards, books at levels students can access independently, writing tools and bookmaking supplies, and plenty of letter manipulatives for word-making activities. Teachers should be observed working with small groups of students breaking spoken words into sounds, matching those sounds to their associated letters, and also doing the reverse—blending letter sounds into words. For emergent bilinguals, it is important that these activities take place with picture or photo cards to enhance comprehensibility.

In 2nd and 3rd grade classrooms, a focus on fluency should be apparent. This means that students should be engaged in reading connected text (not just word lists) for a significant portion of their reading block time. A visitor should hear phrases such as "read with expression" or "read as someone would talk" or "how does that question mark change the way you read that line?" when observing teachers work with students on their fluency. As students advance from transitional to intermediate reading, academic vocabulary and complex language structures that typically hinder meaning-making should be explicitly taught. This should be evident through vocabulary word walls or sentence frames used in lessons, such as "I know that the main characters in this story were _____ because _____." For all levels of readers, teachers need to clearly explain and scaffold strategies for comprehending text so that literacy activities are consistently seen as meaning-driven and purposeful. In other words, teachers ask meaningful questions about students' reading; they don't simply ask them to recall facts.

What evidence indicates that explicit instruction is occurring in a reading or writing lesson based on the core literacy elements? First, the lesson's purpose and focus are clear. Perhaps a student-friendly goal is written or illustrated on the board or on students' papers, or the goal is stated directly by the teacher. When asked, a student can share the learning goal. Even if an educational leader does not have in-depth knowledge of literacy development, key words such as *sounds, letters, fluency, comprehension,* and *vocabulary* will likely stand out and emerge in the discussions they hear or are a part of. In explicit instruction of the core literacy elements, leaders will see instructional personnel modeling word-level, comprehension, and writing skills. Leaders will also see instructors check for understanding of the new learning as described in Chapter 5, provide opportunities for learners' active participation, and share feedback that helps students gauge their progress toward the learning goal (Hattie & Yates, 2014). Finally, there is adequate time in the lesson to address the content, and students are given opportunities to practice or review the new learning. Visitors will see teachers using hands-on materials that contain letters, words, sentences, and passages, and students will be actively using these in their lessons. Students should demonstrate excitement about their literacy learning as they engage with texts, and visitors might hear self-affirmations such as, "I know that letter," "I figured out what that word is by myself," or "That was a great book!"

To advance their literacy skills, emergent bilinguals need the same focus on evidence-based core elements as do all students. The good news is that students who bring literacy from another language with them to school have the potential to kick-start their reading development in English because many reading and writing skills transfer from one language to another. For example, students who already can decode in an alphabetic language understand that letters represent sounds in systematic ways; their new challenge becomes identifying the particulars of how the English writing system is similar to or different from their home language. Teachers should informally assess all of their multilingual students early in the school year so that they can build bridges to students' literate knowledge and bolster success with classroom goals. Similarly, strategies for comprehending text, such as making inferences and identifying themes, can be applied across languages. Knowledgeable teachers support bilingual students to activate literacy knowledge in their home language to support their learning in English (Zapata, Laman, & Flint, 2018).

Emergent Bilinguals Need a Focus on Language and Meaning-Making

All students require focused instruction in the key literacy components, but emergent bilinguals need extra support in language-based comprehension no matter which core element they are working with. Two big pitfalls present themselves when literacy instruction is presented in a generic manner and without concern for the specific needs of language learners. First, students may not possess the vocabulary required to be successful in the reading task. For example, imagine that a beginning reader attempts to sort picture cards into groups with a common vowel sound in the middle. Pictures of *rug* and *nut* will be placed under the *sun* category and *hot* and *frog* will be placed under the *log* category. But what happens when a student cannot identify a picture card such as *mop* or *hut*? This sets up a roadblock to students' learning and full participation in the lesson. To be successful, the teacher will need to take extra time to ensure that language learners can say the name of each picture and thereby distinguish the middle sound. Without the needed vocabulary, the task becomes useless.

Another pitfall emerges when students take part in literacy activities but a focus on meaning is set aside. This might occur in a wide range of activities—for example, a student is asked to sound out words without knowing their meaning; students are asked to read more and more quickly, but their comprehension is never ascertained; or students participate in isolated skills work that is disconnected from any literacy activity in the real world. In these instances, students may come to experience reading as only the decoding gear of the language-word recognition partnership. This misconception can lead to students abandoning their quest to seek meaning in their reading, thus letting go of the purpose of literacy. Over time, this practice will convince students that reading is simply sounding out words, leading them to give up the challenge of making it a meaning-driven process.

If fortifying language is paramount to good literacy instruction for emergent bilinguals, what should instructional leaders advocate and expect to see in classrooms? Vocabulary support, in both the classroom environment and lessons, should be apparent. Physical artifacts could include vocabulary picture/word walls, bilingual dictionaries, digital devices with translation capability, and more. Teaching practices include a preview of vocabulary words used in the lesson, pairing students with a partner who can help interpret new words, embedding active vocabulary learning during a lesson, and frequent and explicit checking for students' understanding. For example, Chapter 5 peeked into Ms. R's 1st grade language arts lesson as her students delved into asking questions about their reading. After her highly scaffolded introduction to the topic, students moved on to working with a partner to ask and answer questions about their independent reading books. To further support language learning, while partner talk took place, Ms. R moved from partnership to partnership, checking in on the conversations among students. When she heard students using the key vocabulary well, she moved on. When the language was not coming as easily, she spent a minute with the partners, sharing the word cards they had reviewed and modeling sentences they could ask each other. Before moving to another team, she guided students to ask and answer their own questions. While practices vary across grade levels, the important thing is for educators always to pair meaning with any reading or writing lesson.

Students Need Time, Practice, and Feedback to Become Proficient

Think back to a skill that you have mastered and feel comfortable doing. Whether that competency is speaking a second language, driving a car, or writing a story, you know the time you invested in learning *how* to do it, trying it out for hours and hours, and having someone help you get better at it. At school, students need the same opportunities to develop proficiency. Practicing important literacy skills at school is not silent, and it is often not solitary. Putting literacy skills into action does not take the form of students facing the teacher and listening to a lecture. What it does look like is students actively reading, writing, asking questions, researching information, discussing books, examining and analyzing words, and listening to interesting texts.

Language learners gain competence by using new language with others, so in a classroom where language and literacy are being acquired, there will be lots of talking and interaction happening. Still, teachers often feel that when a coach or principal enters the room, everything should be quiet and orderly. It is incumbent on instructional leaders to acknowledge that creating opportunities for practice within classrooms does not mean chaos, but it does mean there will be a productive buzz of activity. It is important to be explicit with teachers about this expectation and to help them find ways to provide guided practice as students engage in literacy behaviors that will give them reinforcement opportunities to gain mastery.

Throughout the school day or literacy block, students should have opportunities to engage in a variety of experiences, including: (1) hearing instructors present informational and narrative text beyond the reading level of students (*read to*); (2) reading text at students' personal instructional levels to practice and extend their skills (*read with*); (3) having opportunities to *write* for personal growth or communication; (4) examining how words are constructed in English (*word study*); and (5) processing what they are learning through dialogue (*talk*) (Helman, Bear, Templeton, Invernizzi, & Johnston, 2012). Each of these activities provides opportunities to better understand the varied purposes of literacy, practice skills in meaningful ways, and connect in-class work to the outside world. Regardless of the published program or materials in use, all of these literacy events should take place regularly.

Students do not need to be experts at reading and writing to engage in purposeful and active lessons at school. Kindergarten students can write letters to family members or friends using their best developmental spelling; 2nd graders can use reading and writing to research a topic of interest and share findings with classmates or the community; and 6th grade students can create scripts for multimedia projects or make books to house in the school library. Constructing these authentic lessons may not be as easy as enacting the next page of a teacher's guide, but they are especially valuable for students who need explicit mentoring to connect inside- and outside-of-school literacies. Instructional leaders should applaud when they see students using their literacy skills in purposeful and active ways in classrooms, and let instructors know that they value the scaffolding they have constructed in order to apprentice their students in reading and writing.

Teachers Help Students Connect Inside- and Outside-of-School Literacies

For many emergent bilingual students and their teachers, there may be a wide gap between how reading and writing take place at school and what these activities look like at home or in the local neighborhood. At school, reading often involves the use of texts that share the lives of people who look very different from students' families, use unfamiliar language and formal syntax, and are often read for the purpose of answering questions on a test. In the local neighborhood, reading may look like poring over magazines and newspapers, communicating with friends, following "how to" manuals, and learning from or exploring the Internet.

Teachers who connect students' real lives to the school curriculum find that it serves many purposes. First, students are more motivated when they know that the academic goals in class are useful in the larger world of their communities. Second, materials that reflect people and activities from students' cultural and linguistic backgrounds help students feel connected and provide ready ground for being welcomed into a community of readers and writers. Third, the more familiar the content and style of materials in classrooms are to students' ways of being in the home community, the fewer obstacles will exist to enjoying, engaging with, and understanding the learning goals in class (Lee, 2007).

For teachers to create literacy classrooms that are culturally and linguistically sustaining to students, they must learn about students' outside-of-school experiences, see the backgrounds and experiences of students and their families as assets, and build on students' strengths to advance their academic learning. A good example of this relates to how students' home languages and cultures are valued in class or ignored.

Ms. D wanted to see if reading literature that had characters and scenes representing students' Mexican American life experiences changed the young students' motivation to read and comprehension of the stories. Through her structured inquiry comparing well-known children's literature often found in primary-grade classrooms and books that had won Mexican American book awards, she documented student responses and their ability to more fully engage with the books. She witnessed students' growing ability to connect to literature in ways they hadn't been able to with previous materials in class. Upon first seeing one of the culturally relevant books, one student gasped, "Oooh. This is … this is Mexican!" All of the Latinx (gender neutral alternative to Latino and Latina) students in the group said they were able to identify themselves as being a part of the book (Delbridge, 2018).

Linguistically responsive teachers first learn about the background languages of students through conversation, informal assessments or student work, surveys, or home visits (see Chapter 2 for more on this topic). Next, teachers share appreciation for goals of multilingualism that enable students to participate in diverse discourse communities. Finally, teachers help students use their home languages as a foundation for new learning in English. A classroom with bilingual reference materials and texts, student work posted using multiple languages, posters highlighting ethnically diverse people, and content relevant to typically underserved communities will immediately change the atmosphere and focus for students. Adding to that, teachers can foster an accepting community by being interested in students' languages outside of school, allowing students to use all of their linguistic resources when writing, and reading books that are by and about multilingual people. Inviting in community members from varied linguistic backgrounds to share their literacy histories can be a simple step toward creating an accepting multilingual environment and learning more about students' funds of knowledge and outside-of-school resources (González et al., 2005).

There are numerous ways that instructional leaders can support connections between inside- and outside-of-school literacies throughout the building. To begin, leaders can work to create inclusive schoolwide structures as described in Chapter 4. When leaders set goals and model cultural and linguistic inclusivity at the school level, teachers are more likely to follow suit in their classrooms. Instructional leaders also can design recognition opportunities that highlight students' multilingual literacies, such as bilingual writing contests or displays. Leaders can encourage teachers to learn about how school communities use literacy in purposeful ways and construct professional learning opportunities for staff to brainstorm and share projects that build links to these activities.

Students Are Engaged and Held to High Expectations

Two key findings across numerous research studies in educational settings are that engagement is critical to student learning and that students need to be held to high expectations to be successful (Hattie, 2009). Unfortunately, as an educational leader, you have likely seen many classrooms where these two principles are not in place. Students in classrooms may be asked to sit and listen for long periods of time or do repetitive and inauthentic literacy tasks. Emergent bilingual students may be put on the sidelines and not included in regular classroom activities. Teachers may say that certain students "just aren't ready" for the curriculum or can't learn because their families aren't literate. These negative mindsets are far too common, and it is key for instructional leaders to address them actively and conscientiously.

Educational leaders likely know their staff well and probably have ideas for the best ways to fight back against teachers' low expectations and feelings of lack of efficacy. Certainly, the engagement and high expectation aspects of instructional practice are worthy of focus for ongoing professional learning time and plans of action for school improvement (Maxwell-Jolly & Gándara, 2012). The good news is that collegial discussion and peer observation are some of the most powerful ways to continuously improve in these areas. Instructional staff can observe each other and share what is working to increase student engagement in their classrooms. If one teacher who holds high expectations for students can share his or her voice in a collaborative conversation, other teachers will learn that their students can also be successful.

What techniques might an instructional leader recommend that teachers do to help emergent bilingual students stay engaged in literacy classrooms? Since students can become disengaged when the level of talk is beyond their language comprehension level, it is critical to support student understanding of what is being communicated in class. It is very helpful to have visual resources, such as pictures and procedure charts, that students can use as a backup for instructions that teachers give orally. For example, 3rd grade teacher Ms. N posted numerous charts in her classroom that guided students through the many activities in the day. These included the main components of a story, the difference between a skinny question and one that requires more thought, how to participate in writer's workshop, procedures for word study activities, and a math vocabulary bulletin board. When Ms. N asked students to begin work on a certain type of project, a number of her emergent bilingual students would move to the related visual support chart to follow directions from that.

Structures should be in place for students to work with language partners who can help share instructions in the student's home language. This means that students have been taught how to "turn and talk" in an efficient manner (knee-to-knee or elbow-to-elbow, etc.). For working with a partner outside of the community meeting time, students know who their partners will be and what the expectations are for their work time together. Some teachers pair up newcomer students with a "buddy" who speaks the same home language so that the student always has access to the information being shared in class. A buddy can also be an extra pair of eyes in class to see if new students are understanding information/directions in English or if they need more support. Less-structured partner interactions mean that even when partners are not available who know the student's home language, every class member feels a responsibility to help others understand lesson expectations and support the active engagement of all peers at all times.

In a class with high expectations, students are not isolated while they wait to become more proficient speakers of English. They participate to the best of their ability, and a greater amount of scaffolding is provided so that they can accomplish some aspects of the instructional goal. Expectations are differentiated, but all students are expected to be challenged and give the learning task their full effort. Students are mentored to look out for one another, with the goal being a classroom community in which students support one another's growth.

Within this classroom community, there will be times for small-group work based on the literacy skills or language support that students need. Skill-focused groups are not fixed, however, and groupings are not used as excuses for emergent bilinguals to be regularly separated from the classroom community based on the limits of their language proficiency. Throughout the classroom day, there are opportunities for students to work in heterogeneous groups based on interests or other factors. When grouping is flexible and based on specific academic needs, students know they are being held to high expectations and work to meet those goals.

Summary

Instructional leaders do not need to be literacy experts, but they do need to be assured that the teaching practices occurring on-site are based on research that shows their effectiveness for the students being served. Instructional leaders also need to have a general understanding of how literacy instruction varies depending on students' levels of proficiency in reading and writing. This chapter described a number of key instructional practices and learning opportunities that leaders should expect to find in classrooms across the elementary and middle grades. These practices include using ongoing informal assessment that leads to differentiation in literacy instruction based on students' language and literacy development, prioritizing the importance of language in literacy learning, and explicit instruction for students learning in an unfamiliar language. Students need adequate time and practice to develop mastery and use literacy skills in purposeful and active ways. Teachers should demonstrate high expectations for all students and use their knowledge of what students bring to class to highlight connections to new or demanding material. Instructional leaders help all of these instructional principles become real in classroom settings through their guidance and oversight.

Resources for Further Learning

The following online resources are a good first step to help you gather additional information related to evidence-based practices in the literacy classroom. Each link will lead you to many more resources:

- **Reading Rockets.** This site is a "launch pad" of resources for parents, teachers, school leaders, and others on particular literacy education topics. It contains information on the core literacy components, literacy instruction, reading tips for parents, and much more. A companion site, Colorín Colorado, provides resources in Spanish. Visit http://www.readingrockets.org/.
- **International Literacy Association.** This professional association for literacy educators, instructional coaches, and administrators focused on reading, writing, and communicating is a great source for professional standards, policy statements, and professional materials. Visit https://www.literacyworldwide.org/.
- **Mama Lisa's World.** This site contains hundreds of songs and rhymes from around the world in dozens of languages. It is a great resource for incorporating students' home languages and cultures into the early literacy program by presenting material in both the home language and English simultaneously. Visit https://www.mamalisa.com/.

Evidence-Based Practices in the Content-Area Classroom

As highlighted in Chapter 6, being *literate* in today's world means being able to access increasingly complex texts through both decoding and linguistic processes. Decoding processes allow students to decipher words and attach a verbal representation to them. Linguistic processes call upon students to use their language resources to find meaning in words and interpret the message being presented. The term *literacy* goes far beyond the idea of a set level of proficiency (e.g., "reading at the 3rd grade level"), however. You may find yourself in conversations with educators and community members about mathematical literacy, scientific literacy, historical literacy, computer literacy, geographical literacy, and so many more types. In these cases, *literacy* refers to the ability to understand and engage in the work of an area and to use the language of the field along with the needed communication and record-keeping skills. Some people call these capabilities the *habits of mind* that those who engage in the topic use to accomplish their activities. So, for example, someone who studies history understands that there are competing narratives at any given historical point in time and that it is critical to probe deeply into artifacts from the past to contextualize who created them and for what purposes. The student of history reads primary and secondary sources, uses evidence to corroborate and compare interpretations, and sets forward arguments orally or in writing (Goldman et al., 2016).

As students progress through the elementary grades and into middle school, their literacy learning becomes increasingly contextualized in particular disciplines, such as science, literature, social studies, or mathematics. Over time, coursework tends to be taught more frequently by specialists who are well steeped in their discipline; information tends to be presented through texts or other sources that have dense and complex syntax, highly specialized vocabulary; and advanced concepts that are less likely to be demonstrable through illustrations. This confluence of factors makes the curriculum especially challenging for emergent bilinguals. Add to this dilemma the fact that, unless emergent bilinguals have studied the content previously in their home language, they will primarily be learning these advanced concepts and language simultaneously, so they will likely experience more difficulty callling upon linguistic resources in their home language. For example, *chromosome* is an academic word unlikely to be in common parlance in most household conversations, so students are unlikely to be able to pull from their home language reservoirs.

Teaching and Learning in the Disciplines

To be prepared for college and career, students need to engage in a range of disciplinary literacies, evident in the standards set by a number of professional educational organizations (e.g., National Council of Teachers of Mathematics, National Science Teaching Association). The International Literacy Association (ILA, formerly the International Reading Association, or IRA) published a position paper on adolescent literacy in which it set out eight key principles for student experiences that support advanced disciplinary literacy development (IRA, 2012). These include the following:

- Receiving instruction in the literacy strategies needed in the specific discipline

- Being immersed in a culture of literacy with a systematic and comprehensive program
- Having access to and instruction with multiple and multimodal texts
- Experiencing differentiated instruction based on students' individual needs
- Participating in oral communication during literacy activities
- Using literacy for civic engagement
- Experiencing assessments that highlight students' strengths and challenges
- Accessing a wide variety of print and nonprint materials.

Each of these principles has direct relevance for improving instruction for emergent bilingual students, and numerous examples of these will be explored later in the chapter. While not comprehensive, Figure 7.1 highlights literacy processes used in four disciplinary areas: literature, science, mathematics, and history (Goldman et al., 2016). Learning through disciplinary literacies involves working with advanced terms and discourse structures and more specialized reading and record-keeping routines (Shanahan & Shanahan, 2008). What this process looks like varies greatly across disciplines, however.

Applying Scaffolded Instructional Principles to Disciplinary Literacy

Content-area teachers tend to be specialists in their fields, and their understanding of the subject matter is important. In addition to being knowledgeable in their discipline, these educators should also have pedagogical content knowledge—the awareness of how to teach the subject matter for students at particular levels of development (Shulman, 1986). Unfortunately, some educators behave as if the student must fit the curriculum, as opposed to the curriculum being tailored to the interests and talents of the students. Hearing an instructor say, "Most of the students in my advanced [insert subject matter here] class will fail. They just don't have what it takes" is unacceptable for the profession. Other educators may have a deep desire to engage all their students in the disciplinary literacy curriculum but simply lack the tools for scaffolding their instruction. The upcoming sections of this chapter explore how specially designed instruction takes shape in content-area classrooms, what leaders can look for and encourage, and next steps for strengthening the behaviors subject-matter teachers use in their work with emergent bilingual students.

FIGURE 7.1
Argumentation and Inquiry Within Specific Disciplines

Literary Argumentation and Inquiry	Scientific Argumentation and Inquiry
• Constructing arguments about text meanings • Comprehending characters, motivation, and plots • Interrogating points of view • Valuing interactions among communities of readers	• Generating claims and testing hypotheses • Connecting findings to scientific principles • Considering alternative explanations • Working with communities of similarly engaged scientists
Engaging with Disciplinary Literacies	
Mathematical Argumentation and Inquiry	**Historical Argumentation and Inquiry**
• Using symbolic notation and visual displays of information • Connecting written or oral language with numbers and symbols • Comprehending dense and technical grammatical patterns • Solving problems and presenting proofs • Reviewing and analyzing data in teams or alone	• Understanding interactions among people and events • Placing individual events into larger historical contexts • Generating interpretations by corroborating across historical documents • Engaging with artifacts, documents, and accounts of historical moments

Chapter 5 examined four key ways to tailor instruction for students learning through a new language. In this chapter, the same support principles are used and applied to learning the disciplinary literacies. In the sections that follow, you'll read more about how educators use systematic and explicit instruction, connect to what students know, facilitate student engagement, and build learning communities in their content-area classrooms. Together, these support strategies open worlds of learning and involvement to students who may not yet see how they have a role in these disciplines.

Use Systematic and Explicit Instruction

Chapter 5 explored three big ideas for enacting systematic and explicit instruction in the classroom. These included matching instruction to students' levels of need, presenting content in clear and understandable ways, and providing opportunities for guided practice. These principles are equally valid for upper elementary and middle school students, because the content they are studying takes a quantum leap forward in terms of conceptual complexity and the use of unfamiliar academic language. Moje (2015) explains that it is not useful for students to simply learn the definitions of technical words. The key for them is to apply the language in real disciplinary activities:

> If, however, teachers, school leaders, policymakers, and researchers reconceive of literacy teaching and learning as being about teaching young people the purposeful and meaningful literacy practices engaged by people within and across disciplinary domains, then teachers can embed literacy teaching practice in meaningful ways. Rather than expecting youth to arrive in the classroom with a preexisting motivation to learn a discipline, teachers can apprentice and guide students into their own understanding of the value and purpose of disciplinary reading, writing, and speaking (Moje, 2015, p. 255).

Content-area educators in upper elementary and middle school classrooms can make sure their teaching is matched to students' learning levels by conducting a variety of informal assessments at the beginning of and throughout units of study. These may include quick writes based on a prompt, student self-assessments of their knowledge and interests, and sharing what they know about conceptual vocabulary. Then, differentiated instruction can be provided by adapting the content, learning process, or products to be created (IRA, 2012). For example, prior to introducing a new study of government, the educator might ask students to write down all of the forms of government they can think of and what they believe the labels mean. This activity will help the educator plan instruction that begins at the right place and provides the degree of language scaffolding that will be needed. It is critical that any assessment of student learning be based on multiple measures and, for emergent bilinguals, provide opportunities for sharing what they've learned in multimodal ways.

Many of the strategies for making content clear and understandable have been noted earlier in this book, but they bear repeating because of how important they are for student success. When instructors present information to the group, it is critical that they face listeners, use visuals, stress key words, and frequently check for understanding. For students at earlier levels of English acquisition, language can be modified so that sentences are shortened with superfluous words weeded out. Teaching should be contextualized in real-life examples or experiences using videos, photographs, texts with illustrations, and/or by acting out the task or objective. To provide reference materials for students to access, educators can post vocabulary walls that have illustrations and words for important terms used in the subject matter. Students will also benefit from opportunities to write key vocabulary in a personal notebook and illustrate these terms or use their own language (including their home language) to note what the terms mean.

Educators who model a task before asking students to do it support student learning immensely because there are so many cues the language learner can pick up through observation. Even more helpful is when instructors think out loud as they model the activity. For example, before asking students to reflect on one of their readings in poetry, the teacher might model how to use sticky notes to jot down their thoughts and place the notes on the text. Simultaneously, teachers can use verbal metacognition to share with students what is going on as they reflect, such as, "When I read this line, I thought, I have never heard anyone describe loneliness in that way. The words bring out such sadness; I want to take note of how the author did that."

Instruction can also be made clearer and more understandable by combining oral instructions with written versions. Language learners will rely on a concrete product that they can refer back to throughout the unit of study. Examples of things that should be available to students in writing are directions for assignments, procedures for accomplishing tasks in class, rubrics for grading, components of reference materials (e.g., text features, graphs, indexes, tables of contents), important questions that practitioners in the discipline ask themselves as they work, and tips for identifying valid sources on the Internet, to name a few.

The third big idea for providing systematic and explicit instruction is for educators to structure opportunities for students to practice what they are learning under the guidance of an experienced mentor. Content-area classrooms are places where students learn and practice the behaviors of members of that disciplinary community (IRA, 2012; Moje, 2015). For example, literary communities read, interpret, and discuss literature. Scientists pose questions, collect and analyze data, and share their learnings with others. Historians investigate artifacts that reflect specific times, places, and struggles. Students need these same opportunities to try out disciplinary literacies with the guidance of their instructor. The following list, while not exhaustive, demonstrates many of the ways that educators can provide guided support for students who are learning about and using disciplinary literacy practices in their content-area classes:

- Engaging students in directed reading-thinking activities in which they are guided through a chapter, a textbook, or an article to highlight its text features, make predictions, and discuss how it might be read by someone in the discipline (Stauffer, 1975; Templeton et al., 2015).
- Modeling and practicing how to take notes or record results efficiently.
- Providing explicit instruction in comprehension strategies and then using them collaboratively in group work, such as summarizing key ideas and synthesizing information from various sources (IRA, 2012).

- Identifying important conceptual vocabulary and structuring ways for students to use it in their classwork, such as through writing prompts, text frames, and finding related words (Helman et al., 2017).
- Modeling and practicing doing close reading of short pieces of text (Fisher & Frey, 2019).
- Identifying patterns in the subject matter—whether literature, science, history, or mathematics—and helping students locate their new understandings in relation to the patterns with which they have already worked.
- Using writing prompts to guide students in their use of source materials (Monte-Sano & De La Paz, 2012).
- Working through the complex academic language (syntax and discourse structures) students will experience in their activities as a whole group with modeling and opportunities for student questioning.

Connect to What Students Know

Chapter 5 explored a variety of instructional activities that can be used to learn more about students' previous understandings of the academic content and make connections to what they will learn in class. To expand on these foundational ideas, this section delves into how these strategies for making connections might be used in content-area classrooms. Educators, who bring subject-matter knowledge and knowledge of teaching (pedagogical content knowledge) to their jobs, are then challenged to learn about their students so that bridges can be built that connect students' lives to the activities of a specific disciplinary community. When mathematics teachers understand aspects of students' out-of-school lives, for instance, they can highlight how mathematics may relate to community issues students are aware of. For example, one educator whose community was experiencing a drought and had implemented water restrictions constructed math lessons that used measurement and graphing to learn about how much water is used in various life activities. Students also monitored rainfall and statewide totals and compared these figures across years of data. This learning enabled students to better understand the pressing societal issue they were a part of and invited them to bring data into conversations taking place in their community.

For students to become part of a community of practice of mathematicians, scientists, historians, or any other field, a few things are required: interest, a connection to their lives, a knowledgeable person to guide them, and a sense of competence as they engage in disciplinary activities. How can content-area teachers cultivate these social and emotional competencies? First, they begin each academic study by *activating students' prior knowledge* of the topic. In this process, students make connections to their lived experiences, family stories, texts they have read, or previous interactions with media and technology (Helman et al., 2017; IRA, 2012). For example, a science teacher introducing a climate unit might ask students to recall a time when weather had an impact on their families. Perhaps water leaked into the house during a heavy storm or the family had to cut back on watering the yard during a drought. A connection has now been made, and the educator opens the door to learning about how members of a particular disciplinary community study the issue. The task, then, is to scaffold classroom learning in a way that helps students maintain their interest and see themselves as capable members of the disciplinary community who solve problems and work independently and in collaboration with others.

The following practices help students *feel more competent* and *encourage interest* in the discipline:

- Move from known information to new ideas—the learning load will not overwhelm students at the start.
- Tell the stories of people who work in the field or have made important contributions—in particular, people who represent marginalized communities similar to those of students in class.
- Ask students to brainstorm what they would like to learn and do relating to the topic.
- Stress that it is okay to share misconceptions and learn in collaboration with others. Learning together is a key part of work in a disciplinary community.

- Work on civic engagement projects that are meaningful in students' lives (IRA, 2012).
- Tap into the power of cognates—make connections between technical terms and related words in students' home languages (Helman et al., 2017). Students will feel validated about the out-of-school resources they have to call upon.

As students mature and interact with academic content that is increasingly complex, it is critical that they are aware of the progress they are making—how what they are learning *builds on their previous knowledge and experiences*. Students can show what they have learned by using graphic organizers that visually demonstrate their progress and how their information networks have expanded. Examples of these visuals include concept maps that can be added to over time, story maps that document students' acquisition of disciplinary literacy skills, or double-entry journals to capture new ideas in writing. Students can also review their own pre- and post-assessments, come back to an anticipation guide they completed prior to a unit, or take another look at their self-assessments of vocabulary knowledge and add what they have learned (Templeton et al., 2015). Students also do transformative work when they take ideas learned in class and use new media to communicate their learning. Through each of these activities, students develop self-reflection and are increasingly able to monitor their own understanding and set goals for next steps in the discipline.

Facilitate Student Engagement

Apprenticeship in the disciplinary literacies is an ideal way to call upon the active engagement practices set out in Chapter 5. Students in content-area classrooms desire to *do* more than to simply listen or respond. In literature classes, students want to engage with texts they are interested in and then discuss their reactions and questions with others. In science classes, students want to do the work of scientists—come up with questions, conduct experiments, and analyze what happened and why. Historians want to peek into other times and peoples' lives and make sense of them. Subject-matter instructors can facilitate this by cutting down lecture or passive viewing time and structuring ways for students to become active participants. This does not simply mean setting students loose to do the work on their own. As noted in the discussion of systematic and explicit instruction, educators provide clear guidance as students engage in the practices of the discipline (Moje, 2015). Each step in the learning process—whether working with data, summarizing findings, communicating claims, or producing varied texts—is clearly taught, begins at the level of student need, and is mentored by a knowledgeable guide.

You may associate the following list of classroom activities with a class in the language arts; however, these interactive practices easily extend to other disciplines as well:

- Connect the content being studied with oral stories or literature. Narrative is a pathway into the content for many students.
- Provide choice for students related to which book to read, which problem to tackle, which experiment to conduct, or which model to build. When choice of content is not possible, provide opportunities for students to show their learning in different ways— through hybrid texts, visual presentations, or constructing a model.
- Encourage students to predict, question the material and/or the author, and self-reflect.
- Use writing in a variety of ways: for note-taking, graphing, responses to guided prompts, quick writes, and communication in writing or online forums.
- Write for different audiences: in-class group members, online communities of practice, friends, the school community, families, and the public.
- Expand traditional notions of texts. Include the Internet, story-telling, dance, and visual literacy in class studies.
- Have students identify and sort concepts they are learning to make connections among the technical terms used in the content area (Helman et al., 2017).
- Build discussions in small groups and with partners into classroom routines related to specific disciplinary practices (e.g., team meeting times).

- Use authentic reading materials, primary source material, current events, and problem-based topics to pull students into the material.
- Have students self-assess and create learning portfolios.

Educators who use these and other engagement strategies with students will find that students have greater motivation for in-class learning, identify more as a member of the disciplinary community, and understand the content more deeply. Figure A.5 in the Appendix, an observation guide focusing on engagement and learning, provides a range of date sources to help educational leaders better understand that level of student engagement within disciplinary learning communities.

Build a Learning Community

What can subject-matter educators do to help all of their students, including emergent bilinguals, feel like they belong to the disciplinary community in their classrooms? There are a range of approaches that involve cultivating individuals' identities within the discipline, fostering a safe space for talking and sharing, structuring fun and interactive projects and lessons, and facilitating peer discussions and teacher-student relationships.

A first step for educators to help students feel connected to the discipline could be to conscientiously support their identities as scientists, historians, mathematicians, writers, and so on. At the visible level, buttons, stickers, hats or lab jackets, notebooks with special names, team identities, and more add to the feeling of being part of the community. Going deeper, educators can model and support the behaviors that professionals in the field use as they communicate and interact with students and try out classroom versions of similar activities. For example, writers may need quiet spaces to compose and then time with peers to share their work, ask questions about their writing, and get feedback. Scientists typically pose questions, work in collaborative teams, and discuss their results, so students can follow the steps and procedures professional scientists do. Readers of literature write in reflective journals and have conversations in book clubs or with peers. Students need apprenticeship to feel a part of the field of study they are entering.

As discussed in Chapters 3, 4, and 5, students must feel that the classroom is a safe space to present ideas, make mistakes, and learn from others. Emergent bilinguals will likely need peer translation and supportive conversation to process the material in class. This collaboration should not be seen as "copying," but there should also be procedures in place for students to be included with key responsibilities in school work even when their language skills in English are still developing. Teachers, as classroom leaders, set the tone for inclusion, cooperation, and support within their classrooms. Many students will also be successful with virtual networking and online discussions, whether with peers who speak their home language or simply because online communication gives them more time to put their ideas down in writing.

In the upper grades and middle years, peers become more of a priority at school. Educators can capitalize on students' social natures by including plenty of games and group activities to help students feel connected to others. For example, a vocabulary jigsaw invites students to learn a new concept and terminology in a small group and then teach that concept to other groups (Templeton et al., 2015). Other interactive vocabulary activities might include pair-shares, physical concept sorts, card games, charades, or drawing games using key concepts (Helman et al., 2017, Templeton et al., 2015).

Ultimately, students will feel inspired by educators who show passion for the subject matter and welcome students into the discipline using what they know about students' cultures, languages, interests, and personalities. Figure A.2 in the Appendix, an observation guide focusing on classroom relationships, provides a number of data sources to help educational leaders better understand the quality of relationships within learning communities in content-area classrooms.

What to Look for in a Content-Area Classroom That Supports Emergent Bilinguals

Stepping into Mr. D's 5th grade science class, it is hard at first to identify who is leading the class and what exactly is happening. Students are working in small groups around tables with construction projects in the center. Some students have notebooks and pencils, while others are in the process of building. Some groups have moved away from their tables to use empty floor space. There is a buzz of decentralized discussion taking place, but everyone seems focused on what their team is doing. Steps for the project are on colored paper sheets at each table, and an observer notes that, on the sheets, students have signed up for roles such as team leader, note taker, and materials coordinator. The observer wonders, "Is this a classroom or a laboratory? How did the students learn to do all of this?"

While subject-matter studies vary by level of schooling and disciplinary area, there are many ways that a visitor can look for the kinds of experiences that support language learners to acquire important knowledge and skills while they are still learning English. The sections that follow explore some of what might be evident in the physical environment, educator actions, and student behaviors in linguistically responsive content-area classrooms. Many of these observable artifacts and actions can also be found in the observations guides in the Appendix.

The Physical Environment

The walls of the language-learning content-area classroom provide interesting information about the curriculum that takes place in the room—perhaps an illustration of the water cycle with photographs, arrows, and labels; or maybe it is a mathematics classroom with a math word wall that illustrates and labels mathematical symbols or defines different mathematical operations; or perhaps a wall contains book covers of young adult historical fiction representing dozens of perspectives relating to colonization, immigration, and settlement patterns of the early to mid-1800s. When students look at the classroom walls, they learn new words and concepts through visual displays with labels.

On the whiteboard at the front of the room, learning targets for the day are written in the form of "I can" goals (Tovani & Moje, 2017). For example, in one mathematics class, students aimed for the learning target "I can identify visual models of fractions that are equivalent even when the number of parts is different." In language-learning classrooms, there is evidence of reference materials at students' developmental and linguistic levels—photos, diagrams, charts, illustrations, resource books, computers, and electronic tablets. There are multilingual materials as well, such as bilingual dictionaries and books in languages other than English. On the walls or on the bookshelves, there are opportunities to read about leaders in the discipline who represent the backgrounds of students in class. Classroom norms and procedures for regular activities that take place in class are posted, perhaps with icons or photographs to represent an example of the valued behavior.

Looking around the room, visitors feel as if they are entering a work space that is similar to the environments that people in the disciplinary field use. For example, a literature class appears ready for book groups to meet; a science class has work spaces for collaboration, experimentation, and note-taking; a mathematics classroom is set up for small-group and whole-group problem solving with easy viewing of a group-problem-solving space (e.g., whiteboard), along with plenty of mathematical tools, such as measuring and drawing devices, computers and tablets, and hands-on materials for testing spatial and numeric relationships. In each type of subject-matter classroom, materials that are needed to enact the tasks within the discipline are evident, such as interesting literature and composition books, artifacts from particular time periods, and realia from nature. Students also have access to the "tools of the trade" that help them explore the artifacts, including lab materials, record-keeping devices, books and reference materials, computers, and so on.

Educator Actions

In classrooms where educators facilitate interactive disciplinary literacy learning, visitors will see a range of roles for instructors. At times they present information in short bits but always check for understanding and involve students interactively. As students work on projects, solve problems, or otherwise do the work of the discipline, educators move around the classroom, checking in on groups and offering guidance, information, and support. Following group work, educators facilitate student reflection through debriefing meetings.

Educators who facilitate language learning know how to judiciously present information to their class and do not use "telling" as a teaching strategy. When they lecture, it is for short periods of time (less than 10–12 minutes) and their presentation includes lots of visual information. Teacher talk is broken up by student processing, such as through think-pair-share activities. Depending on the point in the lesson at which visitors enter the room, they might observe the educator providing a clear and explicit opening that shares learning targets and presents information students will need to do the work; guiding the work of students as they enact the disciplinary task; debriefing in collaborative groups or with the whole class; or setting next steps for another lesson (Tovani & Moje, 2017). Some of the language educators use during these lesson components might include the following (Dutro, Núñez, & Helman, 2016; Invernizzi, 2014; Johnston, 2004):

The opening and minilesson:
 Watch while I show you…
 Do that along with me this time.
 Let me explain this chart…
 Say that line with me…
 Notice the learning target for today…
 How might this learning target help you in your life?
 In our last session you… Today we will continue by…
 Here is the plan for the day…
 This is how people…
 This is how your team will be structured…
 What questions do you have about the plan?
 Turn to a partner and discuss what you will do today.
 Signal that you understand the instructions.

During the work session:
 If you get stuck, review the procedure chart.
 What is your plan for the day?
 What could your group do to be more successful?
 What do you notice about…?
 How else could you figure that out?

How will your group accomplish that?

Ask your team members what they think.

What materials do you need?

Whose responsibility is that?

How can you help the notetaker (leader, materials person, etc.)?

What have you learned so far?

Do you agree that…?

What evidence do you have for that idea?

I see you have figured out… What is next?

What kind of problem do we see here?

What surprises you?

I see some good work going on here. You are…

Describe what just happened.

What do you think made that happen?

In what ways does this problem seem similar to what we have studied before?

What other problems does this remind you of?

What is another perspective on that?

How else might a person…?

One of the things people do when they get stuck is…

What if…?

I wonder…

Debriefing:

What are you taking away from today's work time?

How did your work time go today?

What worked well?

What could be improved?

How would you assess whether teammates had equal participation time?

What questions or problems came up? How did you solve them?

How did you know…?

What do you still need to figure out?

How could you check?

How will you use what you learned today outside of class?

What will your next step be?

You will notice that these questions are open ended rather than requiring a simple Yes or No answer. These types of questions elicit higher-order thinking, but they may be challenging for emergent bilinguals at the early levels of English learning. There are several ways that answering open-ended questions might be scaffolded for these students. First, students could work with language partners to ask and answer questions in their home language. If that is not possible, students can answer by drawing or using gestures. Educators can modify questions by offering options for students that make the question more direct, such as changing, "What is another perspective on that?" to "Do you think that someone would think ____ or ____?" It is important that, over time, scaffolds are reduced so that all students are encouraged to use as much language as they can muster, even if they do not use completely correct or academically complex English.

Collaboration among educators such as classroom teachers, specialist teachers, English learner teachers, or other support personnel is another thing that might be evident in a language-learning classroom. A visitor might observe co-teaching wherein the strengths of educators with diverse background knowledge are shared, additional personnel are available to support the guided work taking place, or educators provide focused support to students in smaller groups to learn particular target knowledge or skills.

Student Behaviors

As must be clear from the flow of information so far in this chapter, when visitors enter linguistically responsive content-area classrooms, first and foremost they should see active and engaged students. If students happen to be listening to a presentation, they are *doing* something—frequently sharing with a partner, taking notes, responding verbally or through physical signs, or following the steps of a guided procedure. For example, as Mr. B's 7th grade science class learns about scientific inquiry, he has made a list of key words he wants students to notice in the textbook and his lectures. These words—*experiment, data, variable, observation, investigation, hypothesis, control group, experimental group, qualitative, quantitative, analyze, interpret,* and *predict*—are written prominently on the whiteboard at the front of the room. Students have also written the words on their note-taking sheets. Their task during his lecture is to put a check mark next to each vocabulary word every time they hear it and to add a comment about what they are learning about its meaning. To facilitate his students doing this, Mr. B makes sure that he monitors the use of these key words, slows down his presentation so that students have time to take notes, and periodically checks in on what students have learned about the vocabulary. Most of the time in class, however, students should be doing the work of the discipline, whether that is reading, writing, discussing, illustrating, collecting or analyzing data, solving problems or seeking patterns, conducting research, examining artifacts, or taking part in collaborative projects.

Students demonstrate their knowledge of class norms and guide their peers to behave in collaborative ways. They know that classroom expectations apply to everyone, including themselves, and seek out support from written materials, peers, or instructors when they are confused or need guidance. For example, Kevin Flanigan has found RAFT papers to be an excellent way to engage students in his American history classes. Students write a paper putting themselves into history by selecting a *role* for themselves (e.g., someone who has recently immigrated to the country), an *audience* for the writing, a *format* (e.g., a letter), and a *topic* (e.g., what challenges have been experienced) (Flanigan, Hayes, Helman, Bear, & Templeton, 2017). Studying people throughout history, and the topic of immigration in particular, involves using empathy toward people who may have very different life experiences than what each student has experienced. For this reason, Flanigan outlines classroom norms and helps students practice them so that they coach and respond to one another's papers in thoughtful, nonjudgmental ways, using guiding questions such as, *What feelings might immigrants have? What effect could these experiences have on daily life? What connections can you make to your life right now?* Students are encouraged to probe and understand one another's perspectives and lead their peers to additional perspectives, rather than providing a simplistic assessment.

Students in linguistically responsive classrooms ask questions, use their growing language skills and technical vocabulary to the best of their ability, and ask for help with unknown words or vocabulary. This is apparent when students call upon the academic vocabulary that they see on word walls and cue cards (e.g., "The *trapezoid* has one set of *parallel lines* like this picture.") and ask questions about definitions ("What is that word that means when one company owns everything?").

Students show signs of taking on the identity of an active participant in the discipline, whether as a reader, a writer, an editor, a scientist, a historian, or a mathematician. For example, students in Ms. V's 5th grade language arts class post video book reviews onto their class web page for other students to learn about reading materials that may interest them. In Ms. A's 4th grade mathematics class, students consolidate schoolwide survey data relating to which school lunches are the most popular and present the data to school leaders and food service representatives.

Tips for Strengthening Teaching Behaviors That Support Disciplinary Literacy for Emergent Bilinguals

Based on the principles from the IRA/ILA set forth earlier in this chapter, educators are expected to be knowledgeable in their specific disciplines, know how to teach with multiple and multimodal texts, differentiate their instruction for students' varied needs, guide oral communication in class, plan and enact projects for civic engagement, use varied assessments that guide instruction, and access a wide variety of print and nonprint materials (ILA, 2015; IRA, 2012). These are high expectations for educators, and gaps that may exist at individual school sites cannot be addressed all at once. Each school leader—whether an administrator, an instructional coach, or a lead teacher—will need to work with a team to gather data on current staff strengths and areas for growth that come from self-reflection surveys as well as observational and achievement data (see a variety of observation guides in the Appendix). The following are some potential ideas for helping staff take next steps to support emergent bilingual students in their subject-matter classrooms:

- In teams, have staff examine student learning data to see who could use support in meeting learning targets in their classes. Plan and test approaches for enhancing opportunities for identified students.
- Guide content-area teachers to meet in teams and set goals to make their classrooms more linguistically responsive. Encourage a focus on specific observable strategies and collect data—perhaps by looking at student work products—that can be reviewed at team meetings.
- To help students learn academic language, have educators at specific grade levels meet together to come up with a core set of vocabulary that can be reinforced across content areas. For example, words such as *substance*, *standard, compound, character,* and *evolve* are useful academic words that have different meanings across disciplines. If students study these words in various contexts during their school day, they will increase their vocabulary knowledge in both breadth and depth.
- Gather language prompts that support student thinking, such as the questions and phrases listed in this chapter. Have educators print out these questions on cards for use during their teaching. These language prompts can also be shared concretely with students to help them prepare to answer the questions or so that they can ask them of peers in their group work time.
- Invite literacy specialists to work with all content-area teachers, sharing strategies for disciplinary literacy instruction and brainstorming new ideas together.
- Provide job-embedded professional development, such as coaching, peer observation, or book study, to foster new teaching practices on-site.
- Provide material resources and training for using technology, online networking, and multimodal texts for educators who have yet to use such methods.

Summary

Students at the upper elementary and middle school grades face increasingly complex academic content in their subject-matter classes. Educators at these levels, while knowing a lot about their subject matter, may feel at a loss to scaffold their instruction for students learning in a new language. So that students can be more successful with this advancing disciplinary content, it is important that educators specially design their teaching for relevance and accessibility. This chapter examined ways for educators to assess student learning needs systematically, present content clearly, and guide students to take on the disciplinary literacy tasks in their field. The chapter highlighted a number of ways to connect disciplinary content to students' background experiences through stories, community projects, and sharing personal experiences. Through both active learning lessons and collaborative work, students become more engaged and feel a greater sense of inclusion in the subject matter. The chapter presented many examples of educator language to support student thinking, as well as descriptions of the kind of teaching that will help students acquire deep knowledge in the discipline and put it into action in meaningful ways.

Resources for Further Learning

- **Adolescent Literacy Briefs.** The International Literacy Association (ILA) produced two position papers on the topic of adolescent literacy and the role of content-area teachers in developing disciplinary literacy. To download them, visit
  — https://www.literacyworldwide.org/docs/default-source/where-we-stand/adolescent-literacy-position-statement.pdf.
  — https://literacyworldwide.org/docs/default-source/where-we-stand/ccss-disciplinary-literacy-statement.pdf?.

These briefs contain valuable information about what is needed to support disciplinary literacy for middle and secondary students and present hundreds of recommended resources for further study at the end of the documents.

- **Content-Area Standards from Professional Organizations.** In addition to your state's content-area standards and the Common Core State Standards, visit these professional organization websites to check for guidance about implementation of disciplinary literacy:
  — Next Generation Science Standards: https://www.nextgen-science.org
  — National Council of Teachers of Mathematics: https://www.nctm.org/Standards-and-Positions/Principles-and-Standards/
  — National Council for the Social Studies: https://www.socialstudies.org/standards

Facilitating
Professional Learning

Being an educational professional means striving to get better and better at helping students learn and supporting them to put their knowledge into meaningful action on behalf of their current and future aspirations. Educational leaders have the responsibility not only for continuous learning in education but also for enhancing the schoolwide system and the capabilities of the professionals who work in it. Throughout this book, what it takes for emergent bilingual students to have successful learning experiences at school has been examined. It is unlikely, if not impossible, for any of these educational innovations to become regular components of a school program if there is not cohesion among staff and collaboration for program improvement. For this reason, this chapter focuses on how educational leaders can build the collaborative teams and job-embedded learning opportunities that will ensure that current research findings, contextualized to the local context, turn into regular practices throughout the school.

Although data show that emergent bilinguals are not being served at school as well as students who bring more academic English to school, the research highlights that teachers have not received the coursework that would help them better call upon the strengths, and address the needs, of linguistically diverse students. Most teachers have had minimal formal instruction in how to tailor their pedagogy to support students who bring a language other than English to school (Lucas & Grinberg, 2008) and, because teachers are likely to be monolingual, may not have a thorough understanding of the challenges that emergent bilinguals face (Lucas & Villegas, 2010).

Still, it is not the image of a solitary teacher working tirelessly on behalf of his or her emergent bilingual students that is the primary answer to the question of how best to support student success. As noted throughout this book, in addition to knowledgeable and committed teachers, emergent bilinguals and other culturally and linguistically diverse students succeed when there is alignment between educators and families, when high expectations are set and multiple forms of data are used to measure students' progress, when schools are inclusive and culturally sustaining, and when colleagues team up to provide cohesive learning opportunities schoolwide. Similarly, professional learning is one of the key components of school improvement, but it functions in partnership with the use of data, differentiated and tailored instruction, and cultural responsiveness in systematic ways, as discussed in Chapter 3 (see Figure 3.1).

This chapter explores how educational leaders work with their staffs to facilitate professional learning opportunities that move actual practice on-site closer to the vision embraced by stakeholders. Leaders play an important role in supporting the conditions necessary for meaningful professional learning to take place, including using data in academic decision making, ensuring that research-based methods are implemented, supporting the piloting of promising instructional practices and teaming, and helping staff reflect on what is working or what needs adjustment with students from various demographic groups or with different learning needs (Helman & Pekel, in press). This chapter will also delve into the professional learning community (PLC) structure for collaborative learning: how it is composed, what its objectives are, and what its weekly work could look like. A variety of PLC activities are presented, along with example topics that shine a light on what the work of job-embedded professional learning looks like. The chapter concludes with first steps for designing professional learning with a focus on cultural and linguistic support for students and suggested online resources for further information.

Powerful Professional Learning

It is easy to come up with descriptors of "run-of-the-mill" professional development experiences. They are likely to be short term; not tailored to an educator's school context; not differentiated to participants' background knowledge; and provide limited opportunities for practice, feedback, or reflection. Powerful professional learning, by contrast, is job embedded and addresses the pressing goals of the school community. *Job embedded* means that the focus for the professional learning connects directly to the school improvement plan; that it involves a team of people on-site working for the same outcome; and that there are opportunities for participants to take in information, try out teaching practices, collect and analyze student data, reflect, get support and feedback, and learn from others as they adapt and refine their pedagogical moves. For example, when her school data showed that the same group of students was not meeting grade-level reading benchmarks from year to year to year, Principal Jenna Peters and her school leadership team did a deep analysis of results and theorized about what was getting in the way of making their school vision of equity a reality. They focused their action plan on how to help educators structure teaching in small groups so that students could receive differentiated instruction. Job-embedded professional learning at their site consisted of staffwide analysis of student performance data, conversations and co-teaching between Title I staff and classroom teachers, and professional development on how to manage small-group instruction (e.g., What are the other kids doing?). This long-term and context-specific professional learning had a much greater impact on school improvement than methods that had been used previously.

What Is Required for Meaningful Professional Learning to Take Place

Professional learning has been defined as "experiences that take place within a collaborative culture of shared leadership, that increase educators' knowledge about content and pedagogy, and enable them to use that knowledge to improve classroom and school practices that improve student learning" (Swan Dagen & Bean, 2014, p. 44). Professional learning that has this type of effect for individuals and school communities is not short term or superficial; it requires long-term planning and a substantial use of human and material resources. Figure 8.1 provides a big-picture look at the conditions that support focused professional learning. The next several sections will consider each of these components in turn.

FIGURE 8.1
Supports for Meaningful Professional Learning

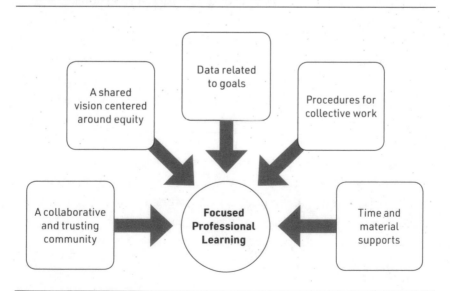

A Collaborative and Trusting Community

As described in Chapter 4, developing trusting relationships is foundational for an inclusive school climate and culture. In addition to creating bonds between educators and students, and between school staff and family members, and helping students develop positive peer-to-peer relationships, the adults at school need to experience high expectations and a safe place to share their strengths and areas for growth. A trusting learning community is not likely to develop if members who share personal uncertainty or examples of failures are met by disparagement or negative professional appraisal. Thus, as is needed schoolwide and in individual classrooms, the adult learning community must uphold norms of listening carefully, keeping what is shared private, being supportive of others' learning, and collaborating to achieve common goals.

A Shared Vision Centered Around Equity

Building the relationships that will support the work of a collaborative culture is a good first step; however, without a focus on student learning and equitable academic opportunities, professional learning will not address the critical issues necessary for school improvement. As described in Chapter 4, the school vision must be created collaboratively with all stakeholders and center around equity for culturally and linguistically diverse students. Collaborative discussions based on student learning data should be used to identify which high-impact aspect of the larger school vision should be concentrated on first and then move forward from there. In the earlier example, Jenna Peters's school chose to focus on helping teachers implement small-group instruction. If a school's vision statement involved validating bilingualism, one goal for professional learning might be for educators to gain a greater understanding of the characteristics of the languages that students speak at home and how these languages are used with their families.

Data Related to Goals

Professional learning should lead to student growth. But without comparable data that can be analyzed among colleagues, opinions rule the conversation. Once a goal for professional learning has been set for the collaborative team, it is incumbent on the group to find or collect data that can be used to assess where students are and investigate instructional practices that help them experience more success. For example, for the goal related to validating students' bilingualism, team members may decide to collect data informally from students in small groups about what languages they speak other than English and in what contexts they use these languages. After gathering these data, team members will meet to share what they learned about students' bilingual strengths and set a learning goal of their own for better understanding one or more of the home languages. This step leads others on a path of continuous learning related to the goal.

Figure 8.2 outlines some of the data that could be collected and used to analyze progress related to six areas of student learning. Data to be called upon will vary from more to less formal depending on the goal area but will always involve looking at comparable data across classrooms so that new learning about teaching extends beyond individual settings.

Procedures for Collective Work

A vision for school improvement has emerged, a supportive community is in place, and data have been collected. What happens next? Another essential component of focused professional learning is to have agreed-upon ways for analyzing the data and turning the findings into actionable next steps with students. Some examples of these procedures might include a protocol for how meeting time is spent in a PLC, a framework for steps in the coaching process, or a worksheet for grade-level teams to decide which students should receive supplemental support in reading or mathematics. For example, the Path to Reading Excellence in School Sites (PRESS) project, through its "Analysis to Action Worksheet," guides teams of educators to identify which students are likely to profit from support in order to reach grade-level benchmarks or, if too many students fall into that range, when a classwide intervention may be appropriate to implement (PRESS, 2016).

FIGURE 8.2
Data to Share in Focused Professional Learning

Student Learning Goal	Data: Formal Assessments	Data: Informal Assessments
Increased engagement	Attendance at school, attendance in special programs or events	Surveys of students or family members; self-evaluations; educator observations of students during class activities; learning portfolios; artifacts of student work
English language development (ELD)	Standardized annual state measures of language development; district screening or progress monitoring measures	Educator observations of student language use in class; audio or video recordings of student language use in class; vocabulary assessments; student oral or written responses to content presented in class (e.g., from a read-aloud book or ability to follow directions); students' and family members' assessment of progress; dictations of students' oral language; oral cloze activities; examination of language content within writing samples
Reading skills	Standardized state or district reading assessments, including those used for ELD; screening and progress monitoring data collected multiple times throughout the year based on grade-level skills and benchmarks	Observations of students' oral reading; running records or miscue analysis; maze or cloze procedures; skills assessments for phonemic awareness, phonics, or comprehension; word sorts; assessments of reading fluency; students' self-assessments and peer coaching feedback; audio or video recordings of student reading
Writing skills	Standardized state or district writing assessments, including those used for ELD	Prompted writing samples; student writing journals; learning portfolios; student self-reflections; artifacts of writing for meaningful purposes
Content area knowledge and use of disciplinary literacies	Standardized state or district assessments in the content area	Pre- and post-assessments of classroom learning goals; evaluation of completed projects; learning portfolios; student self-reflections and self-evaluations

Student Learning Goal	Data: Formal Assessments	Data: Informal Assessments
Bilingual skills	Standardized assessments in languages other than English	Conferences with students or their families about what languages they use in and outside of school, with whom, and in what ways; oral or writing samples in languages other than English; educator observations of students' language use in class or other settings; bilingual writing assignments; input from speakers of students' home language on students' oral, reading, or writing skills in the home language

Protocols are helpful because they support team members to develop and use common language so that they do not have to reinvent the format for each meeting as they pursue more effective instruction. Sample guiding steps for collective work are presented later in this chapter.

Time and Material Supports

The resource that may be the most scarce for school professionals is time to meet. Creating focused professional learning opportunities requires more than just hoping for it or counting on the goodwill of educators to "make room" for them. Team members must have sanctioned time to meet when they are able to think and reflect, whether in a PLC meeting or with a coach to process their observations. Educational leaders at the school and district levels have devised a number of ways to institutionalize collaborative learning, including overlapping prep times, early-release school days, minimizing staff meeting times that do not relate to improving student learning outcomes, and more. Because time to meet is so limited in most schools, it is important that procedures for collaborative practices be clear and implemented cohesively.

A final condition for job-embedded professional learning to flourish is the provision of material support for the venture. This support could be anything from materials used to collect data, such as audio or video recorders, books to read in a book study group, food to serve to family members during a focus group meeting, and many other possibilities. These material supports are likely not very costly, but they demonstrate a commitment to the learning that will take place and the positive impact it will have on student learning.

The Role of Leadership

School leaders promote student learning through their guidance in a number of interconnected domains relating to a school's vision, school-wide norms, equity and cultural responsiveness, instruction and assessment, school community, and professional capacity of school personnel (NPBEA, 2015). Research on the implementation of new practices in a school points to the importance of principal involvement for it to be effective and sustainable (Kam, Greenberg, & Walls, 2003; McIntosh et al., 2014). As noted earlier, rethinking pedagogical approaches and adopting equity-based practices requires deep learning that begins with research and applies it to the local context of each school's community of educators and students. The continuous-improvement process does not happen because of one exceptional teacher or dynamic principal. Focused professional learning must become systematic, and systems don't come together or stay on track without committed leadership.

Standards from various professional organizations highlight the key role of school leaders in creating and supporting professional learning on-site. These roles include developing a culture for collaboration and data-based improvement; bringing stakeholders together to set a vision and goals for the school; and ensuring coherence in curriculum, instruction, and assessment (Dufour & Fullan, 2013; ILA, 2018; NPBEA, 2015). A quick review of Figure 8.1 highlights ways that an ineffective leader could do significant damage to focused professional learning on-site—if there is not a collaborative and trusting community operating, if the leader has not been a part of a shared vision for equity, if there is limited access to data or no expectations for collective work, or if school resources of time and materials are not available, the efforts are unlikely to take root. When, for example, a school experiences frequent changes in the principalship, it is difficult for staff members to maintain coherent progress toward school goals. Key roles of principals for leading change include creating a collaborative vision, structuring schoolwide expectations for using data based on multiple measures, ensuring that research-based instruction takes place, supporting the piloting of promising instructional practices, structuring self-reflection opportunities for staff, using a wide variety of data, and modeling continuous learning (Helman & Pekel, in press; ILA, 2018; Markow, Macia, & Lee, 2013).

A critical component of long-term cohesion in professional learning in a school site is shared leadership (Dufour & Fullan, 2013; Helman & Pekel, in press). Shared leadership involves principals, educators, and other stakeholders taking joint responsibility for being active leaders in schoolwide decisions and systems (Wahlstrom, Seashore Louis, Leithwood, & Anderson, 2010). With shared leadership in place, the loss of one person on the leadership team is less likely to have a devastating impact. When principal Justin Tiarks describes how shared leadership took shape at his diverse urban elementary school, he notes, "My first learning as a new principal was, I still tried to do everything. You simply can't do that. So, I've really been in the business of developing leaders and systems so that they can run independently and then I can support the leader but give them a chance to shine." Through this shared leadership, Tiarks has seen his school experience a cultural transformation with a shared vision of supporting outstanding educators and healthy families.

Leadership teams are often made up of a set of key members: the principal and potentially other administrators; instructional coaches; specialist personnel in special education, English language development (ELD), or bilingualism; grade-level teacher representatives; family and community members; and more. The leadership team sets up procedures and protocols for collaboration and communication, collects and analyzes data from all stakeholders, and works to ensure continuous and high-quality implementation of the initiative (Fixsen, Blase,

Naoom, & Duda, 2015). The team also works to build consensus when clarity is lacking about next steps that should be taken on school and classroom issues. The leadership team, guided by the principal, is like the architect of a construction project. The architect puts together a design that represents a vision that was generated collaboratively, getting more input as needed, and outlining a plan forward to make the vision a reality. The leadership team, like an architect, holds stakeholders together and empowers their actions, while ensuring that the weekly work on-site is moving in the expected direction.

Learning Together Through Professional Learning Communities (PLCs) and Coaching

Two powerful ways to embed professional learning into the daily work of staff members are PLCs and coaching. This section examines some of the ways these learning structures can lead to greater success for linguistically diverse students.

Professional Learning Communities

PLCs are groups of educators who meet regularly to learn about how to better teach their students (Lieberman & Miller, 2008). PLCs are built on the theory that professional learning is complex, takes time, requires inquiry, and relies on both insider and outsider knowledge (Lieberman & Miller, 2014). When surveyed, most schools report that they have PLCs in place, and, in a recent survey, 90 percent said they meet regularly, averaging one time per week (Basileo, 2016). Not surprisingly, though, what takes place during those meetings is highly variable across contexts. Dufour, Dufour, Eaker, and Many (2010) highlight the following features of high-performing PLCs:

- Shared vision and goals based on student learning
- Collaborative culture focused on learning
- An inquiry stance that compares effective practice to the current reality

- Action orientation
- Commitment to continuous improvement
- Focus on results

One specific type of PLC, as described in Chapter 3, is a data team meeting. Data meetings involve grade-level teams of teachers or the school leadership team meeting periodically throughout the school year after screening and benchmark assessment data are available. At these meetings, educators review the data from either universal screening or progress monitoring assessments and identify classrooms and students that are stalling in their progress, before academic problems develop. The goal is to get resources to educators and students who are not receiving adequate support in a timely and focused manner. Educational psychologist and researcher Matthew Burns proposes four steps for data review meetings after screening or benchmark data have been collected (Burns & Gibbons, 2012; PRESS, 2016):

1. Identify the median score for each classroom. Does the median score fall below the district benchmark criterion (e.g., the 25th percentile on a national norm)?
2. Identify which students fall within the at-risk range (e.g., score below the 25th percentile).
3. As a team, discuss the question: Are there any surprises or students that we missed?
4. Among students not yet meeting the benchmark, analyze the available data or plan for further assessment that will help identify their gaps in reading development and the appropriate intervention to address the gaps.

For data review meetings that examine progress monitoring data, Burns recommends the following steps:

1. Identify which students are making adequate progress in their Tier 2 or Tier 3 intervention. Discuss as a team: (a) Should the intervention be continued?; or (b) Should the intervention be discontinued and a transition plan written?

2. Identify which students are not making adequate progress in their Tier 2 or Tier 3 intervention. Discuss as a team: (a) Have the interventions been implemented long enough?; (b) Have the interventions been implemented with fidelity?; (c) Are there modifications we should make to the intervention within the tier?; and (d) Should we change the level of support offered (i.e., change tier)?

3. Discuss as a team: Are there students who were not identified as needing Tier 2 interventions who we should talk about now?

Data meetings should take place at least once a month, with guiding questions changing based on the type of data being reviewed (screening or progress monitoring).

A different type of PLC meeting may be thought of as an *instructional PLC*. In this type of team meeting, educators focus on sharing instructional practices, co-planning lessons, piloting innovations, and collecting data on student learning in relation to the approach. One advantage of learning in a PLC setting is that it brings together staff members with various backgrounds, strengths, and pedagogical knowledge to share practices that work with students within their school setting. Example steps for an instructional PLC meeting are likely to include the following:

**Part One: Planning for a common lesson
and collection of student work**

1. Identify the school goal or standard to be addressed in classroom instruction.

2. Openly discuss successes and challenges in achieving this goal in the past with students. Team members share what has worked.

3. Building on the strengths of the team's previous experiences, develop a lesson plan to implement that includes collecting student work that will demonstrate their understanding of the standard. Student work may include products such as writing samples, completed assignments, or informal assessments.

4. Schedule when the lesson will be implemented and what data will be brought to the next instructional PLC meeting for analysis.

Part Two: Analyzing student work and setting next steps

1. Following implementation of the lesson, teachers bring back the student work they collected and assess the degree to which students were able to meet the standard. It is often helpful to divide the work into three or four categories, such as *below standard, approaching standard, meeting standard,* and *exceeding standard.*

2. Team members discuss differences in how they assessed student work in relation to the standard. Members come to agreement about what meeting the standard looks like.

3. Team members discuss the impact that the common lesson had on supporting learning in the standard area. What worked, and what could have been improved?

4. The group considers ways to provide a new lesson that will support students who have yet to reach the identified benchmark. A follow-up lesson is created for students who need more support.

5. Plans are made for scheduling the follow-up lesson and collecting data to bring to the next instructional PLC meeting.

6. When or if the expertise among group members is waning and they feel the need to bring in outside expertise, a resource such as a knowledgeable person or curricular support materials can be brought in for the team to learn from. After this infusion of information takes place, members should continue to coconstruct lessons, collect student learning data, and analyze and adapt instruction accordingly.

Instructional PLCs should take place on a regular basis, approximately two or three times each month.

To better serve emergent bilinguals, some schools have formed PLCs that facilitate interaction among classroom teachers, ELD teachers, community liaisons, and other specialists. In studies by Frederick (2013) and Ittner (2017), collaborative teams composed of educators with different pedagogical background knowledge, including ELD specialists, joined forces to, in the first case, plan and carry out instruction that was more relevant to the needs of emergent bilinguals and, in the second case, pilot a linguistically responsive reading intervention for emergent bilinguals. Results from both of these studies documented the power of collaborative learning when educators use inquiry and action to improve outcomes for students learning in a new language.

Coaching

A key feature of job-embedded professional learning is that it takes place in relation to the classroom context over time with ongoing feedback and support. One example of professional learning that reflects these characteristics is instructional coaching, a practice that involves observation and discussion of real classrooms, focuses on the current needs of teachers, and builds new knowledge (Swan Dagen & Bean, 2014). When supplemented with follow-up coaching, teachers have demonstrated significant increases in their capacity to implement innovative practices (Elish-Piper & L'Allier, 2010; McCollum, Hemmeter, & Heishh, 2013).

Instructional coaches may be hired to focus on different areas of innovation related to a school or district vision, such as literacy, ELD, math, equity, or diversity. Typically, an instructional coach participates regularly in PLCs, contributing specialized knowledge about their area of expertise and ensuring that the vision for improvement in that area remains at the forefront. Separately, the instructional coach meets with individual educators or pairs to identify their own problems of practice, suggest teaching approaches that are worthy of trying out, and observe and support educators as they implement the new practices. Because a certain vulnerability is required while participating in a coaching relationship, it is important that the person being coached has a trusting and collaborative relationship with the coach, and that the learning process does not become a performance evaluation. It is also important that the coach is not simply knowledgeable about a certain content area; the coach also needs the interpersonal skills necessary to build relationships and facilitate learning conversations that use concrete data (rather than opinion) and are nonthreatening. Coaches working with educators who are studying their own practice or learning to implement new approaches to teaching emergent bilinguals might choose some of the following topics to observe or model:

- In what ways does the educator scaffold instruction for language learners?
- What classroom activities show the most active participation by emergent bilinguals?
- How are culturally and linguistically diverse students represented in the classroom environment?
- What opportunities for use of English or the home language do students have in the classroom?
- How is academic vocabulary taught and supported?
- Focus on a particular strategy related to explicit and systematic instruction or connecting to what students know (e.g., the use of anticipation guides, graphic organizers, or guided practice) and support teachers' use of the practice.
- Keep track of teacher talk time and opportunities for students to be interactive during presentations.
- Conference about students who are not making good progress on classroom benchmarks. Examine student work or assessment data together and propose next steps for instruction for these students.
- Collect observational data on educators' implementation of schoolwide assessments or interventions with emergent bilinguals and provide follow-up feedback.

The current goal, based on the school's vision and continuous-improvement plan, will guide the focus for coaching. A variety of observation guides related to these topics and that can support this work are included in the Appendix.

Most coaching frameworks involve a three-part model of: (1) a planning conference to set up the focus for the classroom visit; (2) an observation or demonstration of teaching with data collection during class time; and (3) a reflection conference to process the data and set next steps. Despite the potential benefits for improving teaching, not all schools and districts have the resources to fund instructional coaches. In these settings, some alternatives to traditional coaching relationships might include peer coaching, coaching by sharing video of teaching during a PLC meeting with colleagues (e.g., lesson study), new-teacher mentoring programs, or co-teaching. The same procedures can be used in these situations to plan for the teaching to be studied, to collect data from the lesson, and to reflect on what worked and what could be adapted for improved student learning.

Example Professional Learning Activities That Focus on Emergent Bilinguals' Success

In this section, several scenarios are presented that are likely to lead to educators' increased awareness of the needs of their emergent bilingual students and development of enhanced skills for instructing them. These examples are simply a few of the many pathways to improved professional capacity for working with language learners. Each school's vision and goals, along with current knowledge of staff, will guide the specific path most relevant for their needs.

Taking a Longitudinal Look at Achievement Data for Emergent Bilinguals

As a variation of the data team meeting, this PLC begins by gathering language and academic data for students working to gain proficiency in English over multiple years. Time is spent reviewing individual student data to look for those who are progressing well, showing incremental progress, or stalling out. Guiding questions for the analysis might include the following:

- What do our assessment materials tell us that adequate progress is for ELD, reading, and mathematics?
- Which students are not progressing well in one or more of these areas? Does language learning seem to impact their progress in reading or mathematics?
- What factors seem to be influencing students who are plateauing and not making good progress from year to year?
- What further data need to be collected to plan for tailored support for these students?

Following this analysis, commonalities among students will likely be discovered that will guide team members to conduct further study on topics such as systematic English language development, academic vocabulary instruction, making content comprehensible, the alignment and coherence of the school curriculum, and so on. A long-term plan would include learning about and trying out teaching practices or interventions to support identified students, debriefing with team members back in the PLC, sharing student work, and potentially receiving coaching on the implemented practices.

Gaining Skills in Culturally Sustaining Teaching

This professional learning opportunity begins by gathering information from cultural insiders, most likely by dialoguing with family or community members or school-community liaisons, or by educators reading and discussing a book on this topic together. For example, at one elementary school, the community outreach staff from the district who shared the cultural and linguistic backgrounds of diverse students were invited in for an informal sharing and Q&A session. The elementary school staff split into groups of six to eight people with one community liaison joining each group. Participants were told that the discussion would be a safe place (without judgment) to ask questions about cultural perspectives they wanted to learn more about. What followed were thoughtful conversations in which the school staff was able to discover why some of their efforts might not be having the success they had hoped for—such as why providing financial support for science camp did not necessarily ensure that all students would attend. Involvement in a PLC designed to support culturally sustaining teaching practices invites members to reflect on and self-assess their classroom practices based on the new information, looking for ways they are culturally compatible or culturally destructive or blind. If an equity coach or a similar support person is available on-site, this is a good time for individual educators to begin to set professional goals on which they can be observed and coached. Peer coaching partnerships are another option for trying out and getting feedback on the implementation of new practices. Another good next step is for the team to collectively select a specific teaching practice that is culturally sustaining: for example, recognizing and validating students' out-of-school literacy behaviors; employ the practice in each person's teaching context; collect artifacts of student work; and bring these to the PLC for further reflection and discussion. One new practice can lead to many more until team members feel more confident in using a significant number of culturally sustaining methods.

Developing Instructional Materials and Analyzing Student Work Together

In PLCs or other collaborative teams, educators have much to learn by codeveloping instructional materials to better serve emergent bilinguals. The codevelopment process allows team members to learn from one another, refine and build on one another's ideas, and enlarge their understandings of students' in- and out-of-school lives (Honigsfeld & Dove, 2016). The first step is to identify a standards-based area of instruction that emergent bilingual students will need tailored instruction to be able to access. The team uses their background knowledge about instructional support strategies (e.g., graphic organizers, step-by-step directions, visuals) to construct clear and engaging materials for a common unit of study. Next, each teacher uses the collaboratively designed materials in class and asks students to complete an assignment associated with the lesson. Artifacts of student learning are collected and shared at the next team meeting, where members describe what worked and what was challenging about the lesson. As experiences are shared, student work is reviewed to see if it demonstrates understanding of the concept being taught. Ideas are collected for how the material and lesson could be enhanced for improved student learning on the next round.

For example, one group of 2nd grade teachers designed a lesson that addressed the following reading standard for literature: Students should be able to compare and contrast two versions of the same story from different authors or cultures. They shared two versions of "Little Red Riding Hood" with their classes—one from the classic fairy tale tradition and the other an updated version that incorporated Spanish words and cultural themes (Elya, 2015). Students filled in a Venn diagram highlighting similarities and differences between the two versions of the stories and then wrote about their experiences of hearing Spanish words in one of the books. Students were invited to embed some Spanish in their own writing process as well. Teachers could see which students included some Spanish in their writing and whether the cultural connections of the modern story enhanced their analysis. Teachers then strategized about how to encourage students' use of multiple languages in future standards-based lessons.

Learning Through Co-Teaching

Co-teaching is a process in which two or more educators collaboratively and intentionally work with a class of students to deliver instruction. Honigsfeld and Dove (2016) have delineated seven basic co-teaching models that educators use for the benefit of emergent bilingual students, some in which both teachers work with the whole class of students and others in which the students are divided between the two cooperating teachers in smaller groups. Co-teaching creates a structure for input to be differentiated depending on the learner's language level, allows for more teacher eyes to be collecting formative assessment data on students so that content is at the right level, and helps to improve lessons because they have been enhanced through partnership. In turn, the process of co-teaching is a deep learning experience for the partner teachers who are informed by each other's background experiences, brainstorm in synergistic ways, and are often able to provide helpful feedback (Honigsfeld & Dove, 2010). In one urban district that was home to a high percentage of immigrant and refugee students, general education teachers at each grade level were partnered with an EL specialist so that they could co-plan and co-teach their language arts lessons. When I observed the educators co-teaching, I saw a number of strategies being used, including one of the educators sitting near students with the most emergent English skills, making sure they understood the lesson content or, at other times, co-presenting the lesson with one educator demonstrating with body language and visuals. On other occasions, I saw one of the co-teachers taking observational notes of the emergent bilingual students as they followed directions and completed the assigned tasks. One of the co-teachers in this district attributed a lot of the students' success to the collaborative model she followed with her partner. She shared, "[We] interact together, and they're not just her kids, they're mine, and that's something that has really worked for us.... The kids feel the relationship."

Co-teaching is a very deep form of professional learning; however, it requires preparation to be successful, including clear procedures for what co-teaching *is* and what it *is not*. School leaders should provide workshops on what the expected parameters for co-teaching are and make sure that ongoing guidance is provided for educators who engage in this collaborative model.

First Steps in Professional Learning That Support Emergent Bilingual Success

The following is a list of recommendations for educational leaders who want to ensure that professional learning opportunities on-site focus on greater staff capacity for meeting the needs of linguistically diverse students:

- Set high aspirations for students who speak languages other than English.
- Prioritize teacher capacity to foster success with students learning English as a top schoolwide goal.
- Identify educator dispositions that may be impeding student success (e.g., a belief that students can't progress until they become fluent in English, a belief that families don't care about students' progress).
- Using performance data, identify an area of inequity for emergent bilinguals at the school to focus on in PLCs or through coaching.
- Use data from students and family members to better understand what is working and what needs adjustment in classroom teaching or schoolwide responsiveness.

- Learn about the languages and cultures of students and their families.
- Create collaborative teams of professionals that include ELD specialists, classroom teachers, instructional coaches, special educators, and others.
- Study your state's ELD standards and identify areas of language development that educators need to understand better.
- Construct materials, design lessons, and examine student work in collaborative teams to call on a variety of linguistically responsive pedagogical approaches.
- Structure curriculum mapping and alignment activities with the staff to ensure that students receive a coherent program of study across classrooms and school years.
- Do not wait to provide supplemental intervention or other supports to emergent bilinguals solely because of their current English language proficiency.

Summary

This chapter focused on how educational leaders use collaborative professional learning opportunities to increase their staff's capacity to serve linguistically diverse students. The chapter highlighted the critical role that leaders play in setting up a collaborative and trusting community, creating a shared vision for equity, ensuring that data guide instructional decisions, supporting the leadership team's procedures for collective work, and allocating time and material supports to enable the work in teams. The chapter described two important forms of job-embedded professional learning—PLCs and coaching—and suggested topics of inquiry that could be used in these processes. Concrete examples were shared that could guide the work of school staffs to become more responsive and knowledgeable in their teaching of emergent bilingual students.

Resources for Further Learning

Consider pursuing some of the following online sources to learn more about how to facilitate shared leadership and regularize job-embedded professional learning on-site:

- **National Implementation Research Network (NIRN).** Visit the NIRN website to find out more about implementation science—the study of what is needed for innovations to become regularized into routine practice. The site contains background information, research on implementation drivers, learning materials, self-assessment materials, and connections to projects across the country that are striving to improve the uptake of evidence-based practices into the daily work of practitioners. Visit https://nirn.fpg.unc.edu/.
- **PLC Self-Assessment.** Here you can take a free online self-assessment quiz to identify potential next steps for improving the way PLCs function at your school. The site is sponsored by the publishing company Solution Tree, which produces a wide variety of materials for implementing PLCs. Visit https://www.solutiontree.com/plc-navigator/.
- **Resources for Guiding Change.** A number of online resources are available for leaders to reference, share with the leadership team or staff, and help direct their efforts in supporting effective and focused professional learning on-site. See, for example:
  - NCLE (National Center for Literacy Education): Visit http://www.ncte.org/library/NCTEFiles/About/NCLE/NCLEshortlitreview.pdf for a concise review of the evidence behind collaborative teacher inquiry.
  - LOCI (Literacy Organizational Capacity Initiative): Visit http://www.norc.org/PDFs/LOCI/District%20Capacity%20White%20Paper_2018.pdf to read suggestions for how a leader can build instructional capacity among staff.
  - Learning Forward: Visit https://learningforward.org/standards-for-professional-learning to learn more about Learning

Forward's Standards for Professional Learning and access resources for professional learning that leads to improved teaching, leadership, and student results.

— MDE (Minnesota Department of Education): Visit https://education.mn.gov/MDE/dse/prev/res/ to access the Resources for School Leaders page with links to background information, white papers, and organizations to help lead initiatives and share leadership.

— The Academy for Co-Teaching and Collaboration: Visit https://www.stcloudstate.edu/soe/coteaching/default.aspx to learn more about the research on coteaching, its benefits, and how to structure it at your school. Managed by St. Cloud State University in Minnesota.

9

Assessing Your Progress Through an Equity Lens

Each chapter in this book has highlighted an aspect of educational practice relevant to the success of emergent bilingual students, capturing what is essential for educational leaders to know and support within their learning communities. For students from culturally and linguistically diverse backgrounds to thrive at school, equity must be the guiding framework and benchmark of accomplishment. This chapter will explore some of the ways that educational leaders can use data to assess their progress in better serving students who are marginalized because of their backgrounds and experiences, such as speaking languages other than academic English, possessing limited socioeconomic resources, or being persons of color. *Equity* is not something that can be accomplished once and for all. It requires continuous effort and never-ending attention—there is no finish line. Nonetheless, progress toward making school programs more equitable must be documented, analyzed, interrogated, and improved, and this can happen only with the use of evidence. For this reason, this chapter suggests a variety of pathways to help educational leaders document their movement on the journey of fostering success for students from diverse backgrounds.

The chapter begins with a review of the concept of *equity audits*, a structured way to evaluate opportunity gaps for students within a school or district, and one form of highlighting inequities that can later be addressed. Next, the chapter shines a light on the importance of student learning data and surveys to support enhanced equity on-site and reconnects with suggestions from previous chapters about how family and community input can be solicited and used. The final pathway for assessing progress involves documenting growth on educators' professional learning plans and school improvement goals. The chapter concludes with several resources that educational leaders may find useful in their ongoing work to assess progress through an equity lens.

Equity Audits

An inclusive framework, such as the one that guides this book, does not locate the source of inequitable achievement in students or their families. After all, it is the responsibility of educators and school systems to ensure that all students receive access to high-quality instruction, resources that build on what they know, and support in achieving rigorous learning goals. Historically, equity audits were embedded in accountability systems that prioritized reduction in "achievement gaps" in formulized ways (Skrla, Scheurich, Garcia, & Nolly, 2004); however, in the past several years, a greater focus has been placed on *opportunity gaps*, the inequities that students from culturally and linguistically diverse and other marginalized populations experience at school, such as less-qualified teachers, less-enriched curricula, less access to technological resources, and more (Irvine, 2010; Milner, 2012). Scott (2001) uses the term *systemic equity* to describe the antidote to opportunity gaps—structural ways that school systems provide every learner with the resources needed to achieve excellence.

In a recent reconceptualization of equity audits, educational stakeholders collect data that can lead them to better understand concrete opportunity gaps and inequities present in their schools (Skrla et al., 2004). After analyzing the data, they discuss and select potential solutions to address the inequities, and then monitor and evaluate the effects of these approaches (Skrla et al., 2004). Some of the categories and potential data sources for identifying and addressing these opportunity gaps are as follows:

- *Teacher quality.* Do students from marginalized backgrounds have the same access to high-quality teachers as students from non-marginalized populations? Data sources could include connecting students' demographic information to teachers' educational preparation, years of teaching, certification in the subject matter, mobility, and whether or not they represent students' racial and linguistic backgrounds (Skrla et al., 2004).

- *Equity across program involvement.* Do students from marginalized backgrounds participate disproportionately in special education, gifted and talented programs, bilingual classrooms, enrichment opportunities such as music or art programs, academic intervention support, or student discipline systems? Data sources could include lists of participating students disaggregated for demographic data, attendance records, and disciplinary action notes and records, including record-keeping of the time students have been excluded from class.

- *Access to enriched curriculum.* Are students from marginalized communities subjected to a narrowed and monotonous curriculum at their grade level that focuses primarily on success at test taking or learning discrete skills that are repetitive and mind-numbing? Data sources could include lesson planning notes; observations of classrooms at work; stories and photos of classrooms that participate in community action projects, multilingualism, or thematic study; or demonstrations of classroom learning in creative ways, such as through theater, music, dance, art, building, experimenting, and other forms of production and holistic activity.

- *Access to up-to-date learning materials and technology.* Do students from marginalized communities have access to technology, print and digital texts, recent textbooks, and hands-on tools for studying the disciplinary literacies? Data sources could include observations of the learning materials within classrooms, school programs, and library-media centers; purchasing records from school budgets; demonstrations and products of student learning; and attendance records for after-school and enrichment programs.

Equity audits can be conducted using data from an individual school or across a school district or state. They highlight systemic inequities, which should be addressed. For example, if a school community uncovers inequities in which students are losing learning time due to disciplinary exclusion, or if it comes to light that two schools in a district do not have the same technological resources as the others, this is the first step in ameliorating the inequity. Data should be shared with transparency so that the concern does not remain hidden. Issues that surface should be discussed among all stakeholders, prioritized, and emphatically addressed by the leadership team in the continuous school improvement process.

Learning From and About Students

Student achievement data are also used as an element of an equity audit. Typically, this occurs through state-led accountability processes and is based on student scores on standardized yearly assessments. Yearly achievement data, whether for academic progress or language development, are an important yet incomplete source of data on how a school is doing in serving all of its students in equitable ways. The standardized data provide a big-picture snapshot of the results of inequitable learning opportunities. They do not, however, provide much guidance for how to improve. Following are some suggestions for gathering information from and about students that can support program improvement and strengthen inclusion in the school community:

- *Assessment data.* Formative assessment data from classroom teachers and program specialists can provide triangulation to confirm or question results from standardized assessments and screening measures that identify students for tiered interventions.

- *Surveys.* Surveys of students, including picture formats used with the youngest students, let educators know aspects of schooling that students feel are working best for them, what motivates them, what they do outside of school, what they like to read, how well they know a word or a concept, what unit of study they are most interested in learning about, what their personal goals are, how included they feel in the learning community, and so much more.
- *Academic self-assessment and goal setting.* These are two ways for educators to learn about how students see their own strengths and challenges at school. When student goals are aligned with school goals, the results can be powerful. Students become more motivated and feel that the school is working on their behalf, and educators understand students in deeper ways and gain a more comprehensive picture of their evolution as learners.
- *Student voice.* Student voice can be systematically included by creating seats on committees for student members, creating student government bodies, regularizing student-led activities, allowing students to vote for schoolwide events or classroom topics of study, and more. It is important to attend to the makeup of student participants on committees and always consider which student voices are missing from this input or conversation.

Learning from Families and Communities

Chapter 2 explored the importance of gathering information from families and communities to guide program development and improvement. Figure 2.1 highlighted the key approaches to gathering input from families and members of students' cultural and linguistic communities: engaging in listening activities, visiting homes and the community, collecting feedback via surveys and questionnaires, and encouraging participation in school decision making.

To assess a school's progress on better serving all of its students, the visits, listening activities, surveys and questionnaires, and inclusion of people from marginalized communities in decision-making processes can be tailored for formative assessment. The following questions can provide important data for self-evaluation and continuous improvement:

- In what ways do you feel the school is doing better this year at meeting the needs of your child?
- In what ways do you feel the school is not doing as well this year at meeting the needs of your child?
- Here is a list of what the school most wants to accomplish this year. Please put these goals in order according to how important you feel they are (1 is most important; 6 is least important).
- What do you think would most help your child be successful at school?

Collecting data from families and communities does not always need to be a formal process. An open-ended suggestion box or a graph where selections can be added with a colored dot or sticky note in the school hallway can get a sample of responses to prompts such as, "What my child talks most about concerning the school day...." It is critical that all surveys, requests for information, and listening activities be available to people who speak languages other than English.

Documenting Progress on Educator and Schoolwide Goals

An important concept that came up in previous chapters was that of setting a school vision for equity and delineating goals to make that vision come to life. If, however, the school vision is not a working document that is referenced continually, it will lose meaning. For this reason, when data are collected to measure progress for schoolwide equity, the data must be linked to the specific schoolwide goals from which they came. For example, a school that sets a goal for including more linguistically diverse family members on schoolwide committees will need to measure that goal by the growth in numbers of linguistically diverse participants. A goal of increasing public recognition of bilingualism will require gathering data that demonstrate progress, such as the number of students receiving a bilingualism certificate, a "bilingual student of the month" award, or documentation of student learning in more than one language. To keep up the school staff's motivation related to reaching the school vision, artifacts of growth toward meeting a schoolwide goal should be evident in the hallways, staff room, and individual classrooms on campus. For example, if a schoolwide goal is to increase the use of culturally diverse children's literature, bulletin boards can feature these books in classrooms, hallways, and libraries; the staff room could provide information on a featured author of the month; educators could share reflections of how they used culturally diverse literature in a classroom activity; and so on. These actions build momentum for greater commitment and more transparency concerning progress on the goal.

In a similar manner, data should be collected regularly that highlight agreed-upon goals for the work of professional learning communities (PLCs) on-site. These data are often artifacts of student learning related to a new teaching approach or focus of instructional inquiry. For example, a 2nd grade PLC team set a goal of increasing students' writing stamina and collected student writing samples to analyze as they simultaneously tried out innovative teaching approaches over a period of four weeks. Each week the writing data were analyzed according to a set of standards-based criteria during regular PLC meetings. Teachers can keep a portfolio or reflective journal that highlights their progress and challenges in working toward the school vision and goals. A group portfolio can be constructed for teachers working together in a PLC or book club to document their professional learning and the effect it has on students over time. Data may also include evidence collected from classroom observations with a focus on the key areas outlined in the guides presented in the Appendix. Vision leads to goals, goals to action, action to data gathering, and data analysis to replication or revision, depending on the outcome. And, whenever innovation and progress are found, they are celebrated collaboratively with the whole school community.

Summary

This chapter focused on ways that a school community can assess its progress in implementing a vision of equity for students from culturally and linguistically diverse backgrounds. Baseline data can be collected through the use of equity audits that identify how learning opportunities can be enhanced for marginalized students. Important data can also be gathered by looking at student learning and motivation through standardized and formative assessment, student self-evaluation, surveys, and goal setting. Families and communities are essential to assessing progress toward an equitable environment with learning opportunities that support all students. Also critical is the collection of data that connect directly with goals set in the schoolwide plan and in teachers' professional learning collaboratives. Without data, it is impossible to understand what works to improve learning for emergent bilinguals and other marginalized students. With data in a variety of forms, progress takes shape and can be built upon.

Resources for Further Learning

The following websites provide information that may be useful in assessing schoolwide progress on a vision for equity:

- **Intercultural Development Research Association (IDRA).** This nonprofit organization is aimed at achieving equal opportunity for every child through strong public schools. Online resources include position papers and action frameworks, podcasts and webinars, newsletters, and online community engagement. Visit https://www. idra.org/.

- **Californians Together: Championing the Success of English Learners.** This statewide advocacy network of educational organizations focuses on equitable outcomes for all students, including their development of cross-cultural skills, literacy in more than one language, technological literacy, and strong connections to their families. Resources on the website include downloadable educational reports, podcasts and videos, and links to other media and information. Visit https://www.californianstogether.org/.

- **Center for Urban Education, University of Southern California.** The center and its website provide information about educational equity and racial justice through blogs, research articles, and videos. A grant-funded project involves development of a tool that identifies equity-minded indicators. Visit https://cue.usc.edu/.

APPENDIX

What to Look for When Visiting Classrooms

In this Appendix, a number of key characteristics of effective instruction are presented through a series of simple observation guides that can be easily referenced by educational leaders who hope to gather foundational information about what is taking place in their school's classrooms. The guides are not meant to be all-inclusive; rather, they provide a big-picture view of what to look for related to relationship building (see Figure A.2), an enriched physical environment (see Figure A.3), language support (see Figure A.4), and engaging teaching practices (see Figure A.5) during a classroom visit. Figure A.1 provides a sample of how an educational leader might use one of the guides.

An observer would most likely focus on one area at a time, or even one subsection of an area, in a short 10- to 15-minute visit. For example, if a school goal is related to cultural and linguistic inclusion, the visitor might choose to collect data on the people represented on classroom walls and text, whether the topics of study are connected to students' out-of-school lives, and the presence of languages other than English, as noted in Figure A.3—Focusing on the Physical Environment.

Each observation guide highlights key areas that should be present in a classroom that supports emergent bilinguals' success. To the right of the key feature are examples of the kinds of data that could be collected to document what is happening in class. For example, to learn more about teacher-student relationships in a classroom, an observer could collect data on the interactions of the teacher with students, the language and body language the teacher uses, how the teacher responds to student questions, and so on. The observer could also collect data on students' observed comfort level in talking with the teacher. Data should be collected without interpretation or value judgment. In other words, instead of noting, "Teacher did a good job connecting with students," the observer would be better able to have a conversation later if the data were objective. For example, the teacher's language could be scripted verbatim. Or every time the teacher used a student's name, that could be written down. Follow-up conversations will be much clearer if data, not opinions, have been recorded.

At the bottom of each observation guide is a beginning list of questions that could be used to have a more robust conversation on the topic at a later time. These are open-ended questions that are likely to lead to rich and in-depth pedagogical conversations. These questions can be adapted according to each school's vision and professional learning plan.

FIGURE A.1

An Observation Focused on Language Development

This observation guide shares an example of how an instructional leader might document language development during a short 15-minute classroom observation. It is based on Figure A.4—Focusing on Language Development.

What to Look for	Possible Sources of Data	Observations Minilesson, 9:10–9:25
In addition to the focus areas suggested here, physical artifacts, such as agendas, objectives, vocabulary word walls, and labeled visuals, are good sources of data about how language learning is supported in the classroom.		Classroom space included a vocab word wall related to habitats (sun, soil, shelter, food, etc.) and headphones for story listening. Agenda was posted on whiteboard.
Modifying language	Teacher behaviors: • Use of body language • Use of visuals, charts, and realia • Speed, volume, articulation, and direction of speech • Rephrases, simplifies complex language structures • Clarifies unknown vocabulary words Student behaviors: • Questions asked • Ease or difficulty of following directions and responding appropriately	The teacher (T) pointed to agenda and posters while outlining goals for the day. Clarified meaning of "characteristic." T repeated directions for two students (Ss) when they needed it. Ss listened and made eye contact. Ss raised hands when they had questions / / / / / / (6 times total).
Vocabulary instruction	Teacher behaviors: • Previewing or reviewing vocabulary for emergent bilinguals • Language used to explain unknown vocabulary • How much time is spent in the lesson addressing unknown vocabulary • How key vocabulary are identified • Language used to check for understanding Student behaviors: • Language use while exploring new words • How students communicate that they need vocabulary support • Activities students engage in to learn new words	Focus of discussion was preparing for a science lesson to follow (habitats and what animals need to survive). New vocabulary included shelter, air/oxygen, and "depend on." T presented a hand motion to represent each new vocabulary word. Ss made that motion when the word was said (shelter looked like a little cave).

(continues)

FIGURE A.1

An Observation Focused on Language Development—(*continued*)

What to Look for	Possible Sources of Data	Observations Minilesson, 9:10–9:25
Teaching academic language structures	Teacher behaviors: • List of language structures being taught • Techniques for language teaching • Language used to explain unknown syntax Student behaviors: • Language used while engaging with new syntactical structures • Activities students engage in to learn new language structures	T asked students to turn to a partner and state, "A ____ depends on ____ to live." (A bear depends on shelter to live.) All students participated when asked to share with a partner.
Comparing languages	Teacher behaviors: • Questions asked about differences across languages • Connections made between English and other languages students know • Use of multilingual charts, visuals, texts, cards, and websites Student behaviors: • Use of languages other than English in speech and writing • Language used when comparing languages	Didn't observe any. In partner sharing, two groups of students used their home language after sharing the English sentence.
Opportunities to practice language	Teacher behaviors: • How student talk is built into lesson • Balance of teacher and student talk time • Ways student talk is elicited/invited Student behaviors: • Student opportunities to talk (e.g., partner sharing, small-group discussion, one-at-a-time sharing in large group) • Language used by students according to each type of group setting • Which peers students have opportunities to talk with	Primarily teacher talk, but students invited to raise their hands for questions and twice had the opportunity to turn to a partner and share.

Questions for later discussion:

• *Which students need the most support in language development, and how do you provide that support?*
• *How do students communicate that they don't understand the language being presented?*
• *How are students' home languages called upon in the classroom?*
• *How do you balance teacher talk and student interactions?*

After school we discussed what was observed in the morning. The main question we addressed was how T knows which students need language support. T described her background knowledge about students' language levels and her encouragement that students raise their hands when they are not following her language. She is considering adding some kind of hand signal for students to subtly let her know they need clarification. She was encouraged by the engagement that partner sharing brought to students and hopes to use them even more. She also mentioned her desire to write the sentence frame (e.g., A ___ depends on ___ to live.) on the whiteboard so that students could make an oral language–to–print connection.

FIGURE A.2

Focusing on Classroom Relationships

A safe and positive classroom community is foundational for student success. Although relationships are not typically evaluated on checklists, there are certainly ways for an educational leader to get a basic sense of the safety and social inclusion of adults and students in the classroom. This observation guide provides some initial ways to look for this.

What to Look for	Possible Sources of Data
	In addition to the focus areas suggested here, physical artifacts, such as norms for being a member of the learning community and disciplinary tracking charts, are good sources of data about how relationships take shape in the classroom.
Teacher-student relationships	Teacher behaviors: • Personal interactions, saying hello and goodbye, use of students' names • Use of inclusive language or not ("we," "our community," etc.) • Tone of voice and body language used • If and how responses are elicited from all students • If and how disciplinary policies lead to student exclusion • Responses to student perspectives • Responses to student errors Student behaviors: • Level of comfort in asking questions or sharing information • Interpersonal contact with teacher
Peer relationships	Student behaviors: • Language used in personal interactions among students • Collaborative or exclusionary practices of students • Tone of voice and body language used
Adult-to-adult relationships	• Language used in personal interactions between adults, use of names • Tone of voice and body language used • Relationship structure (collaborative, top-down, parallel/independent, etc.)

Questions for later discussion:
• *How have you built positive relationships with your students?*
• *How do you know if this has been effective or not?*
• *In what ways do students experience threat or safety in the learning community?*
• *How is teamwork structured among the adults in the classroom?*

FIGURE A.3

Focusing on the Physical Environment

The contents and layout of each classroom will vary depending on how many students it serves, what is taught, and the aesthetics of the teacher. Nonetheless, all classrooms should allow for safe access to learning materials, the opportunity to interact with peers and educators, learning about the content being studied, and seeing one's self and experiences reflected in the space. This observation guide points out some of the things educational leaders should look for when gathering information about a classroom's physical environment.	
What to Look for	**Possible Sources of Data**
In addition to the focus areas suggested here, physical artifacts, such as agendas and posted procedures and objectives, are good sources of data about what materials are available to students and how they can access them.	
Layout and access to learning tools	• Record of the print and digital writing tools and spaces available to students • Posted expectations for how students access materials and centers • Available meeting spaces in class (e.g., meeting circle, small-group, independent work) • Reference materials that students can access (e.g., alphabet strips, computers)
Learning materials	• Variety of print and digital texts in the classroom • The range of difficulty levels of reading materials • Hands-on materials related to the content area (e.g., scientific equipment or primary source historical artifacts) • Bilingual dictionaries or vocabulary cards • The content represented on classroom walls and its visual clarity
Cultural and linguistic inclusion	• The people represented on classroom walls and texts • Whether the topics of study are connected to students' out-of-school lives • Presence of languages other than English
Products of student learning	• Artifacts of student learning represented on classroom walls and bookshelves • Photographs of students or their work • Student-authored communications
Questions for later discussion: • *How have you constructed an environment that provides access and opportunity to the learning material for all students?* • *In what ways do students see themselves and their communities represented in the classroom?* • *How is multilingualism supported in the classroom?* • *How are materials used to differentiate instruction for language learners?*	

FIGURE A.4

Focusing on Language Development

Emergent bilinguals are learning English as they learn the academic content within their classrooms. For this reason, all teachers of language learners need to consistently integrate language teaching throughout their school day. Instructional leaders can use this observation guide to collect data on how this scaffolding is going.

What to Look for	Possible Sources of Data
In addition to the focus areas suggested here, physical artifacts, such as agendas, objectives, vocabulary word walls, and labeled visuals, are good sources of data about how language learning is supported in the classroom.	
Modifying language	Teacher behaviors: • Use of body language • Use of visuals, charts, and realia • Speed, volume, articulation, and direction of speech • Rephrases, simplifies complex language structures • Clarifies unknown vocabulary words Student behaviors: • Questions asked • Ease or difficulty of following directions and responding appropriately
Vocabulary instruction	Teacher behaviors: • Previewing or reviewing vocabulary for emergent bilinguals • Language used to explain unknown vocabulary • How much time is spent in the lesson addressing unknown vocabulary • How key vocabulary is identified • Language used to check for understanding Student behaviors: • Language used while exploring new words • How students communicate that they need vocabulary support • Activities students engage in to learn new words
Teaching academic language structures	Teacher behaviors: • List of language structures being taught • Techniques for language teaching • Language used to explain unknown syntax Student behaviors: • Language used while engaging with new syntactical structures • Activities students engage in to learn new language structures

What to Look for	Possible Sources of Data
Comparing languages	Teacher behaviors: • Questions asked about differences across languages • Connections made between English and other languages students know • Use of multilingual charts, visuals, texts, cards, and websites Student behaviors: • Use of languages other than English in speech and writing • Language used when comparing languages
Opportunities to practice language	Teacher behaviors: • How student talk is built into lesson • Balance of teacher and student talk time • Ways student talk is elicited/invited Student behaviors: • Student opportunities to talk (e.g., partner sharing, small-group discussion, one-at-a-time sharing in large group) • Language used by students according to each type of group setting • Which peers students have opportunities to talk with

Questions for later discussion:

• *Which students need the most support in language development, and how do you provide that support?*
• *How do students communicate that they don't understand the language being presented?*
• *How are students' home languages called upon in the classroom?*
• *How do you balance teacher talk and student interactions?*

FIGURE A.5
Focusing on Engagement and Learning

This observation guide draws attention to a set of key components to look for during a classroom visit and how they could be concretely discerned. In a brief visit, it would be difficult to see all of these data sources because a lot depends on where in the lesson structure the visit is. At the beginning of the lesson, a visitor would be more likely to observe a teacher introducing the plan for the lesson and sharing content. The visitor could look for clarity, checking for understanding, and the way teacher talk time is structured. Midway through a lesson or unit, a visitor is more likely to get a good sense of inclusion, differentiation, guided practice, and coaching. An educational leader who wants to collect quick data on the school as a whole may focus on only one element and move from class to class with that focus (e.g., In what ways do students experience choice across the school?).

What to Look for	Possible Sources of Data
	In addition to the focus areas suggested here, physical artifacts, such as agendas and posted procedures and objectives, are good sources of data about the specific lesson and overall structure of instruction in the classroom.
Clarity and explicitness of instruction	Teacher behaviors: • Vocabulary and language structures used • Use of visuals and realia • Speed, volume, articulation, and delivery of speech • Ways complex material is clustered in understandable chunks Student behaviors: • Questions asked • Ease or difficulty of following directions and responding appropriately
Inclusion	Teacher behaviors: • Classroom seating arrangement • Grouping of students in homogeneous or heterogeneous groups • Forms of collaboration used • Ways the teacher calls upon students Student behaviors: • Interaction patterns among students
Checking for understanding	Teacher behaviors: • Questions the teacher asks about student understanding of the content or processes being presented • Nonverbal routines for students to share any confusions (e.g., color-coded cue cards, hand signs) • The frequency of check-ins on student understanding • Protocols the teacher uses to keep track of students' learning status Student behaviors: • Student products of their understanding (e.g., exit tickets, actions, or verbal responses)

What to Look for	Possible Sources of Data
Building on what students know	Teacher behaviors: • Language that inquires into students' experiences and connects that to the current topic • Grouping strategies used in class so that more students have opportunities to share • Evidence of family and community resources being used in class Student behaviors: • Use of language other than English in the classroom (written or oral) • Student products that highlight previous and current learning (e.g., K-W-L charts, reflection journals)
Differentiation	Teacher behaviors: • Grouping strategies to provide smaller group instruction (e.g., centers, workshop model) • Structures used to deliver instruction to meet students' needs • The closed or open-ended nature of assignments (e.g., fill in the blank versus journal entry) Student behaviors: • Variation in the materials being used by students • Variation in the time students are able to spend on their work
Guided practice	Teacher behaviors: • Lesson plans provide time for students to work with support prior to doing tasks independently • Teacher actions and language while students try out new skills—watching, providing feedback, answering questions, reminding, coaching, and so on Student behaviors: • What students are doing during the lesson: listening to teacher presentation, practicing with support, or using their learning independently
Coaching for higher-level thinking	Teacher behaviors: • The interaction formats used (e.g., I-R-E [initiate, response, evaluate], whole-group discussion, small-group discussions, partnerships) • The quality of questions and turn-taking in discussions with students • The range of students the teacher is able to interact with • Questions posted on the walls, on procedure charts, in student notebooks, and on assignments Student behaviors: • Language used in peer-to-peer interactions

(continues)

FIGURE A.5

Focusing on Engagement and Learning—(*continued*)

What to Look for	Possible Sources of Data
Moderate and well-paced teacher talk time	Teacher behaviors: • Lesson timing—how much time is spent with the teacher presenting and students listening versus student discussion and activity • How the teacher integrates questioning and student activity into lecture time
Skills are connected to meaningful activities	Teacher behaviors: • Materials used in lessons (e.g., skill centered, such as letter cards, or more holistic, such as books) • Use of language relating to how skills relate to real-world practices • Demonstrations of how skills relate to real-world practices
Choice is provided	Teacher behaviors: • Directions for activities Student behaviors: • Variation in the materials students use • Variation in the activities students take part in • Students describe their projects and assignments • Artifacts of student learning show diversity in form and content

Questions for later discussion:

• *What strategies did you use for student engagement, and how do you think they turned out?*
• *How did your knowledge of students' background experiences and language strengths lead you to believe the lesson was at their instructional levels?*
• *How can you tell if students are able to understand the instruction and participate well?*
• *What are your goals for increasing student engagement?*

BIBLIOGRAPHY

American Institutes for Research. (2014). *RTI essential components worksheet.* Center on Response to Intervention at AIR. Retrieved from https://rti4success.org/sites/default/files/RTI_Fidelity_Rubric_Worksheet.pdf

Anderson, R. C., & Pearson, P. D. (2002). A schema-theoretic view of basic processes in reading comprehension. In P. D. Pearson, R. Barr, M. L. Kamil, & P. B. Mosenthal (Eds.), *Handbook of reading research* (Vol. 1, pp. 255–291). New York: Routledge.

Arias, M. B., & Morillo-Campbell, M. (2008). *Promoting ELL parental involvement: Challenges in contested times.* Education Policy Research Unit, Arizona State University. Retrieved from http://www.greatlakescenter.org/docs/Policy_Briefs/Arias_ELL.pdf

Au, K. H. (2016). Culturally responsive instruction: Application to multiethnic, multilingual classrooms. In L. Helman (Ed.), *Literacy development with English learners: Research-based instruction in grades K–6* (pp. 20–42). New York: Guilford Press.

Baker, S., Lesaux, N., Jayanthi, M., Dimino, J., Proctor, C. P., Morris, J.,..., & Newman-Gonchar, R. (2014). *Teaching academic content and literacy to English learners in elementary and middle school* (NCEE 2014-4012). Washington, DC: National Center for Education Evaluation and Regional Assistance (NCEE), Institute of Education Sciences, U.S. Department of Education. Retrieved from https://files.eric.ed.gov/fulltext/ED544783.pdf

Basileo, L. D. (2016). *Did you know? Your school's PLCs have a major impact.* Learning Sciences International. Retrieved from https://www.region10.org/r10website/assets/File/PLC-Report.pdf

Berg, A. C., Melaville, A., & Blank, M. J. (2006). *Community and family engagement: Principals share what works.* Coalition for Community Schools, Institute for Educational Leadership. Retrieved from http://www.communityschools.org/assets/1/AssetManager/CommunityAndFamilyEngagement.pdf

Bialystok, E. (2007). Acquisition of literacy in bilingual children: A framework for research. *Language Learning, 57,* 45–77.

Bishop, R. S. (1990). Mirrors, windows, and sliding glass doors. *Perspectives, 6*(3), ix–xi.

Blank, M. J., Berg, A. C., & Melaville, A. (2006). *Growing community schools: The role of cross-boundary leadership.* Washington, DC: Coalition for Community Schools.

Blank, M. J., Melaville, A., & Shah, B. P. (2003). *Making the difference: Research and practice in community schools.* Coalitions for Community Schools. Retrieved from https://files.eric.ed.gov/fulltext/ED499103.pdf

Boser, U., Wilhelm, M., & Hanna, R. (2014). *The power of the Pygmalion effect: Teacher expectations strongly predict college completion*. Center for American Progress. Retrieved from https://files.eric.ed.gov/fulltext/ED564606.pdf

Burns, M. K., & Gibbons, K. (2012). *Implementing response-to-intervention in elementary and secondary schools: Procedures to assure scientific-based practices*. New York: Routledge.

Burns, M. K., Pulles, S. M., Helman, L., & McComas, J. J. (2016). Assessment-based intervention frameworks: An example of a Tier 1 reading intervention in an urban school. In S. L. Graves & J. Blake (Eds.), *Psychoeducational assessment and intervention for ethnic minority children: Evidence based approaches* (pp. 165–182). Washington, DC: American Psychological Association.

Chhuon, V., & Wallace, T. L. (2012). Creating connectedness through being known: Fulfilling the need to belong in U.S. high schools. *Youth and Society, 46*(3), 379–401.

Cummins, J. (1979). Cognitive/academic language proficiency, linguistic interdependence, the optimum age question and some other matters. *Working Papers on Bilingualism, 19*, 121–129.

Datnow, A., Lasky, S. G., Stringfield, S. C., & Teddlie, C. (2005). Systemic integration for educational reform in racially and linguistically diverse contexts: A summary of the evidence. *Journal of Education for Students Placed at Risk, 10*(4), 445–453.

Deák, G. O. (2014). Interrelations of language and cognitive development. In P. Brooks and V. Kampe (Eds.), *Encyclopedia of language development* (pp. 284–291). Thousand Oaks, CA: Sage.

Dearing, E, Kreider, H., Simpkins, S., & Weiss, H. (2006). Family involvement in school and low-income children's literacy performance. *Journal of Educational Psychology, 98*(4), 653–664.

Delbridge, A. E. (2018). *Mainstream and Mexican American-themed picture books and students' responses to them in a first-grade, dual-immersion classroom* (Unpublished doctoral dissertation, University of Minnesota).

Dufour, R., Dufour, R., Eaker, R., & Many, T. (2010). *Learning by doing: A handbook for professional learning communities at work*. Bloomington, IN: Solution Tree.

Dufour, R., & Fullan, M. (2013). *Cultures built to last: Systemic PLCs at work*. Bloomington, IN: Solution Tree.

Dutro, S., Núñez, R., & Helman, L. (2016). Explicit language instruction: A key to academic success for emergent bilinguals. In L. Helman (Ed.), *Literacy development with English learners: Research-based instruction in grades K–6* (2nd ed., pp. 43–77). New York: Guilford Press.

Elish-Piper, L., & L'Allier, S. (2010). Examining the relationship between literacy coaching and student reading gains in grades K–3. *The Elementary School Journal, 112*, 83–106.

Elya, S. M. (2015). *Little roja riding hood*. New York: G. P. Putnam's Sons/Penguin.

Ferguson, C. (2008). *The school-family connection: Looking at the larger picture*. Austin, TX: National Center for Family and Community Connections/SEDL. Retrieved from http://www.sedl.org/connections/resources/sfclitrev.pdf

Firestone, W. A., & Mangin, M. M. (2014). Leading professional learning in districts with a student learning culture. In L. E. Martin, S. Kragler, D. J. Quatroche, & K. L. Bauserman (Eds.), *Handbook of professional development in education* (pp. 319–338). New York: Guilford Press.

Fisher, D., & Frey, N. (2019). Best practices in adolescent literacy instruction. In L. M. Morrow & L. B. Gambrell (Eds.), *Best practices in literacy instruction* (6th ed., pp. 150–172). New York: Guilford Press.

Fixsen, D. L., Blase, K. A., Naoom, S. F., & Duda, M. (2015). *Implementation drivers: Assessing best practices.* National Implementation Research Network (NIRN). Chapel Hill: Frank Porter Graham Child Development Institute, University of North Carolina Chapel Hill.

Flanigan, K., Hayes, L., Helman, L., Bear, D. R., & Templeton, S. (2017). *Words their way with American history Volume 1: The world before 1600 to American imperialism (1890-1920).* Boston: Pearson.

Frederick, A. R. (2013). *A case study of a first-grade teacher team collaboratively planning literacy instruction for English learners* (Unpublished doctoral dissertation, University of Minnesota).

Gallo, S. (2017). *Mi padre: Mexican immigrant fathers and their children's education.* New York: Teachers College Press.

Garcia, E. E. (1993). Language, culture, and education. *Review of Research in Education, 19,* 51–98.

Garcia, M. E., Frunzi, K., Dean, C. B., Flores, N., & Miller, K. B. (2016). *Toolkit of resources for engaging families and the community as partners in education: Part 4: Engaging all in data conversations* (REL 2016–153). Washington, DC: U.S. Department of Education, Institute of Education Sciences, National Center for Education Evaluation and Regional Assistance, Regional Educational Laboratory Pacific. Retrieved from https://ies.ed.gov/ncee/edlabs/regions/pacific/pdf/REL_2016153.pdf

García, O., Johnson, S. I., & Seltzer, K. (2017). *The translanguaging classroom: Leveraging student bilingualism for learning.* Philadelphia: Caslon.

Gay, G. (2010). *Culturally responsive teaching: Theory, research, and practice.* New York: Teachers College Press.

Gibbons, K., Brown, S., & Niebling, B. C. (2019). *Effective universal instruction: An action-oriented approach to improving Tier 1.* New York: Guilford Press.

Goldenberg, C. (2013). Unlocking the research on English learners. *American Educator, 37*(2), 4–11. Retrieved from https://www.aft.org/sites/default/files/periodicals/English_Learners.pdf

Goldman, S. R., Britt, M. A., Brown, W., Cribb, G., George, M. A., Greenleaf, C., Lee, C. D., Shanahan, C., & Project READI. (2016). Disciplinary literacies and learning to read for understanding: A conceptual framework for disciplinary literacy. *Educational Psychologist, 51*(2), 219–246.

González, N., Moll, L. C., & Amanti, C. (2005). *Funds of knowledge: Theorizing practices in households, communities, and classrooms.* New York: Routledge.

Gough, P. B., & Tunmer, W. E. (1986). Decoding, reading, and reading disability. *Remedial and Special Education, 7,* 6–10.

Gruenert, S., & Whitaker, T. (2015). *School culture rewired: How to define, assess, and transform it.* Alexandria, VA: ASCD.

Gutierrez, K. D., & Rogoff, B. (2003). Cultural ways of learning: Individual traits or repertoires of practice. *Educational Researcher, 32*(5), 19–25.

Hakuta, K. (2018). The *California English learner roadmap: Strengthening comprehensive educational policies, programs, and practices for English learners* (CA EL roadmap). Sacramento: California Department of Education.

Hakuta, K., Butler, Y. G., & Witt, D. (2000). *How long does it take English learners to attain proficiency?* The University of California Linguistic Minority Research Institute (Policy Report 2000-1). Retrieved from https://web.stanford.edu/~hakuta/Publications/%282000%29%20-%20HOW%20LONG%20DOES%20IT%20TAKE%20ENGLISH%20LEARNERS%20TO%20ATTAIN%20PR.pdf

Hanover Research. (2017). *Closing the gap: Creating equity in the classroom.* Retrieved from https://www.hanoverresearch.com/wp-content/uploads/2017/06/Equity-in-Education_Research-Brief_FINAL.pdf

Hattie, J. (2009). *Visible learning: A synthesis of over 800 meta-analyses relating to achievement.* New York: Routledge.

Hattie, J., & Yates, G. (2014). *Visible learning and the science of how we learn.* New York: Routledge.

Helman, L. (2012). *Literacy instruction in multilingual classrooms: Engaging English learners in elementary schools.* New York: Teachers College Press.

Helman, L. (2016). *Literacy development with English learners: Research-based instruction in grades K–6.* New York: Guilford Press.

Helman, L., Bear, D. R., Templeton, S., Invernizzi, M., & Johnston, F. (2012). *Words their way with English learners: Word study for phonics, vocabulary and spelling* (2nd ed.). Boston: Pearson.

Helman, L., Cramer, K., Johnston, F., & Bear, D. R. (2017). *Words their way: Vocabulary for elementary mathematics.* Boston: Pearson.

Helman, L., Ittner, A., & McMaster, K. L. (In press). *Assessing language and literacy with bilingual students: Practices to support English learners.* New York: Guilford Press.

Helman, L., & Pekel, K. (In press). Literacy leadership: The principal's role. In R. M. Bean & A. Swan Dagen (Eds.), *Best practices of literacy leaders* (2nd ed.). New York: Guilford Press.

Helman, L., Rogers, C., Frederick, A., & Struck, M. (2016). *Inclusive literacy teaching: Differentiating approaches in multilingual elementary classrooms.* New York: Teachers College Press.

Henderson, A. T., & Mapp, K. L. (2002). *A new wave of evidence: The impact of school, family, and community connections on student achievement.* Austin, TX: National Center for Family and Community Connections/SEDL. Retrieved from https://www.sedl.org/connections/resources/evidence.pdf

Herber, H. (1978). *Teaching reading in content areas* (2nd ed.). Englewood Cliffs, NJ: Prentice Hall.

Hofstede, G. (1997). *Cultures and organizations: Software of the mind.* London: McGraw-Hill.

Honigsfeld, A., & Dove, M. G. (2010). *Collaboration and co-teaching: Strategies for English learners.* Thousand Oaks, CA: Corwin.

Honigsfeld, A., & Dove, M. (2016). Collaborative practices to support implementation of the Common Core State Standards with K–5 English learners. In L. Helman (Ed.), *Literacy development with English learners: Research-based instruction in grades K–6* (2nd ed., pp. 282–308). New York: Guilford Press.

ILA (International Literacy Association). (2015). *Collaborating for success: The vital role of content teachers in developing disciplinary literacy with students in grades 6–12.* Newark, DE: Author.

ILA (International Literacy Association). (2018). *Standards for the preparation of literacy professionals 2017.* Newark, DE: Author.

Invernizzi, M. (2014). Critical thinking about vocabulary. In *Vocabulary their way: Words and strategies for academic success, Grade 7 teacher edition* (pp. T18–T23). Boston: Pearson.

IRA (International Reading Association). (2012). *Adolescent literacy: A position statement of the International Reading Association.* Newark, DE: Author.

Irvine, J. J. (2010). Foreward. In H. R. Milner (Ed.), *Culture, curriculum, and identity in education* (pp. xi–xvi). New York: Palgrave Macmillan.

Ittner, A. C. (2017). *Creating a linguistically-responsive intervention for developing readers: A formative experiment with a teacher study group* (Unpublished doctoral dissertation, University of Minnesota).

Jennerjohn, A. (2017). *The principal's role in school-family-community partnership* (Unpublished master's thesis, University of Minnesota).

Johnston, P. H. (2004). *Choice words.* Portland, ME: Stenhouse Publishers.

Jones, S., & Vagle, M. D. (2013). Living contradictions and working for change: Toward a theory of social class-sensitive pedagogy. *Educational Researcher, 42*(3), 129–141.

Kam, C., Greenberg, M. T., & Walls, C. T. (2003). Examining the role of implementation quality in school-based prevention using the PATHS curriculum. *Prevention Science, 4*, 55–63.

Khalifa, M. (2012). A *re-new-ed* paradigm in successful urban school leadership: Principal as community leader. *Education Administration Quarterly, 48*(3), 424–467.

Ladson-Billings, G. (2009). *The dream-keepers: Successful teachers of African American children.* San Francisco: Jossey-Bass.

Lee, C. D. (2007). *Culture, literacy, and learning: Taking bloom in the midst of the whirlwind.* New York: Teachers College Press.

Lesaux, N. K., & Marietta, S. H. (2011). *Making assessment matter: Using test results to differentiate reading instruction.* New York: Guilford Press.

Lieberman, A., & Miller, L. (2008). *Teachers in professional communities: Improving teaching and learning.* New York: Teachers College Press.

Lieberman, A., & Miller, L. (2014). Teachers as professionals: Evolving definitions of staff development. In L. E. Martin, S. Kragler, D. J. Quatroche, & K. L. Bauserman (Eds.), *Handbook of professional development in education* (pp. 3–21). New York: Guilford Press.

Lin, M., & Bates, A. B. (2010). Home visits: How do they affect teachers' beliefs about teaching and diversity? *Early Childhood Education Journal, 38*(3), 179–185.

López-Robertson, J. (2017). Their eyes sparkled: Building classroom community through multicultural literature. *Journal of Children's Literature, 43*(1), 48–54.

Lucas, T., & Grinberg, J. (2008). Responding to the linguistic reality of mainstream classrooms: Preparing all teachers to teach English language learners. In M. Cochran-Smith, S. Feiman-Nemser, & J. McIntyre (Eds.), *Handbook of research on teacher education: Enduring issues in changing contexts* (3rd ed., pp. 606–636). Mahwah, NJ: Lawrence Erlbaum Associates.

Lucas, T., & Villegas, A. M. (2010). The missing piece in teacher education: The preparation of linguistically responsive teachers. *National Society for the Study of Education, 109*(2), 297–318.

Mapp, K. L., & Kuttner, P. J. (2013). *Partners in education: A dual capacity-building framework for family–school partnerships.* Austin, TX: SEDL. Retrieved from http://www.sedl.org/pubs/framework/FE-Cap-Building.pdf

Markow, D., Macia, L., & Lee, H. (2013). *The MetLife survey of the American teacher: Challenges for school leadership.* New York: MetLife Insurance Company. Retrieved from https://www.metlife.com/about/corporate-responsibility/metlife-foundation/reports-and-research/survey-american-teacher.html

Marzano, R. J. (2003). *What works in schools: Translating research into action.* Alexandria, VA: ASCD.

Maxwell-Jolly, J., & Gándara, P. (2012). Teaching all our children well: Teachers and teaching to close the achievement gap. In T. B. Timar & J. Maxwell-Jolly (Eds.), *Narrowing the achievement gap: Perspectives and strategies for challenging times* (pp. 163–186). Cambridge, MA: Harvard Education Press.

McCollum, J. A., Hemmeter, M. L., & Heishh, W. Y. (2013). Coaching teachers for emergent literacy instruction using performance-based feedback. *Topics in Early Childhood Special Education, 33*, 28–37.

McFarland, J., Hussar, B., Wang, X., Zhang, J., Wang, K., Rathbun, A., Barmer, A., Forrest Cataldi, E., & Bullock Mann, F. (2018). *The condition of education 2018* (NCES 2018–144). U.S. Department of Education. Washington, D.C: National Center for Education Statistics. Retrieved from https://nces.ed.gov/pubs2018/2018144.pdf

McIntosh, K., Predy, L. K., Upreti, G., Hume, A. E., Turri, M. G., & Mathews, S. (2014). Perceptions of contextual features related to implementation and sustainability of school-wide positive behavior support. *Journal of Positive Behavior Interventions, 16*, 29–41.

Meyer, J. A., & Mann, M. B. (2006). Teachers' perceptions of the benefits of home visits for early elementary children. *Early Childhood Education Journal, 34*(1), 93–97.

Milner, H. R. (2012). Beyond a test score: Explaining opportunity gaps in educational practice. *Journal of Black Studies, 43*(6), 693–718.

Moje, E. B. (2015). Doing and teaching disciplinary literacy with adolescent learners: A social and cultural enterprise. *Harvard Educational Review, 85*(2), 254–278.

Monte-Sano, C., & De La Paz, S. (2012). Using writing tasks to elicit adolescents' historical reasoning. *Journal of Literacy Research, 44*(3), 273–299.

Morris, E. W., & Perry, B. L. (2016). The punishment gap: School suspension and racial disparities in achievement. *Social Problems, 63*, 68–86.

Morrison, P. (2017). Strawberries in Watsonville: Putting family and student knowledge at the center of the curriculum. In E. Barbian, G. C. Gonzales, & P. Mejía (Eds.), *Rethinking bilingual education: Welcoming home languages in our classrooms.* Milwaukee, WI: Rethinking Schools.

NAESP (National Association of Elementary School Principals). (n.d.). *The principal's guide to building culturally responsive schools.* Retrieved from https://www.naesp.org/sites/default/files/NAESP_Culturally_Responsive_Schools_Guide.pdf

NICHD (National Institute of Child Health and Human Development). (2000). *Report of the National Reading Panel* (NIH Publication No. 00-4769). Washington, DC: Author.

NPBEA (National Policy Board for Educational Administration). (2015). *Professional standards for educational leaders 2015.* Reston, VA: Author.

OECD (Organisation for Economic Cooperation and Development). (2018). *Equity in education: Breaking down barriers to social mobility.* Paris: PISA, OECD Publishing. doi:10.1787/9789264073234-en

Paredes, M. (2010). Academic parent-teacher teams: Reorganizing parent-teacher conferences around data. *Family Involvement Network of Educators (FINE) Newsletter, 2*(3).

Retrieved from https://archive.globalfrp.org/publications-resources/browse-our-pub-lications/academic-parent-teacher-teams-reorganizing-parent-teacher-conferences-around-data

Paris, D. (2012). Culturally sustaining pedagogy: A needed change in stance, terminology, and practice. *Educational Researcher, 41*(3), 93–97.

Philp, J., & Duchesne, S. (2016). Exploring engagement in tasks in the language class-room. *Annual Review of Applied Linguistics, 36*, 50–72.

PRESS (Path to Reading Excellence in School Sites). (2016). *Intervention manual* (2nd ed. update). Minneapolis, MN: Author.

Raphael, T. E., Vasquez, J. M., Fortune, A. J., Gavelek, J. R., & Au, K. (2014). Sociocul-tural approaches to professional development: Supporting sustainable school change. In L. E. Martin, S. Kragler, D. J. Quatroche, & K. L. Bauserman (Eds.), *Handbook of professional development in education* (pp. 145–173). New York: Guilford Press.

Rodríguez, D., Carrasquillo, A., & Lee, K. S. (2014). *The bilingual advantage: Promoting academic development, biliteracy, and native language in the classroom.* New York: Teach-ers College Press.

Scarborough, H. S. (2001). Connecting early language and literacy to later reading (dis)abilities: Evidence, theory, and practice. In S. B. Neuman & D. K. Dickinson (Eds.), *Handbook of early literacy research* (pp. 97–110). New York: Guilford Press.

Scott, B. (2001). Coming of age. *IDRA Newsletter.* Retrieved from https://www.idra.org/resource-center/coming-of-age/

Shanahan, T., & Beck, I. L. (2006). Effective literacy teaching for English-language learners. In D. August & T. Shanahan (Eds.), *Developing literacy in second-language learners: Report of the National Literacy Panel on language-minority children and youth* (pp.415–488). Mahwah, NJ: Erlbaum.

Shanahan, T., & Shanahan, C. (2008). Teaching disciplinary literacy to adolescents: Rethinking content-area literacy. *Harvard Educational Review, 78*(1), 40–59.

Shapiro, E. (n.d.). Tiered instruction and intervention in a Response-to-Intervention model. RTI Action Network. Retrieved from http://www.rtinetwork.org/essential/tieredinstruction/tiered-instruction-and-intervention-rti-model

Shatz, M., & Wilkinson, L. C. (2010). *The education of English language learners: Research to practice.* New York: Guilford Press.

Shulman. L. (1986). Those who understand: Knowledge growth in teaching. *Educational Researcher, 15*(2), 4–14.

Skrla, L., Scheurich, J. J., Garcia, J., & Nolly, G. (2004). Equity audits: A practical leader-ship tool for developing equitable and excellent schools. *Educational Administration Quarterly, 40*(1), 133–161.

Stauffer, R. G. (1975). *Directing the reading-thinking process.* New York: Harper & Row.

Swan Dagen, A., & Bean, R. M. (2014). High-quality research-based professional develop-ment: An essential for enhancing high-quality teaching. In L. E. Martin, S. Kragler, D. J. Quatroche, & K. L. Bauserman (Eds.), *Handbook of professional development in education* (pp. 42–63). New York: Guilford Press.

Templeton, S., Bear, D. R., Invernizzi, M., Johnston, F., Townsend, D., Flanigan, K., Hel-man, L., & Hayes, T. (2015) *Vocabulary their way* (2nd ed.). Boston: Pearson.

Tovani, C., & Moje, E. B. (2017). *No more telling as teaching: Less lecture, more engaged learning.* Portsmouth, NH: Heinemann.

USDE (United States Department of Education)/NCES (National Center for Education Sta-tistics). (2017). *Table 204.20. English language learner (ELL) students enrolled in public elementary and secondary schools, by state: Selected years, fall 2000 through fall 2015.* Retrieved from https://nces.ed.gov/programs/digest/d17/tables/dt17_204.20.asp

Valdés, G. (2001). *Learning and not learning English: Latino students in American schools.* New York: Teachers College Press.

Vygotsky, L. (1978). *Mind and society: The development of higher mental processes.* Cambridge, MA: Harvard University Press.

Wahlstrom, K. L., Seashore Louis, K., Leithwood, K., & Anderson, S. E. (2010). *Investigating the links to improved student learning: Executive summary of research findings.* New York: The Wallace Foundation.

Weiss, H. B., & Lopez, M. E. (2011). Making data matter in family engagement. In S. Redding, M. Murphy, & P. Sheley (Eds.), *Handbook on family and community engagement* (pp. 21–26). Lincoln, IL: Center on Innovation and Improvement. Retrieved from http://www.schoolcommunitynetwork.org/downloads/FACEHandbook.pdf

Weiss, H., Lopez, M. E., & Caspe, M. (2018). *Carnegie challenge paper: Joining together to create a bold vision for next generation family engagement.* Global Family Research Project. Retrieved from https://globalfrp.org/Articles/Joining-Together-to-Create-a-Bold-Vision-for-Next-Generation-Family-Engagement-Engaging-Families-to-Transform-Education

Wentworth, L., Kessler, J., & Darling-Hammond, L. (2013). *Elementary schools for equity: Policies and practices that help close the opportunity gap.* Stanford, CA: Stanford University, Stanford Center for Opportunity Policy in Education.

WIDA. (2013). *RTI2: Developing a culturally and linguistically responsive approach to response to instruction and intervention (RTI2) for English language learners.* University of Wisconsin System: Author. Retrieved from https://www.uab.edu/education/esl/images/WIDA_RtI2_forELLs.pdf

Zapata, A., Laman, T. T., & Flint, A. S. (2018). Language arts learning in multimodal and multilingual contexts. In D. Lapp & D. Fisher (Eds.), *Handbook of research on teaching the English language arts* (2nd ed., pp. 359–383). London: Routledge.

INDEX

Note: The letter *f* following a page number denotes a figure.

ABOUT THE AUTHOR

Lori Helman, PhD, is a professor of curriculum and instruction at the University of Minnesota, where she is also director of the Minnesota Center for Reading Research. She received her master's degree in education administration and supervision and her doctorate in curriculum and instruction (literacy education). During her career, she has been a bilingual elementary school teacher, a district literacy coordinator, a new-teacher program development leader, a teacher educator, and an educational researcher. Helman currently teaches and mentors graduate students, literacy specialists, and future teachers at the University of Minnesota, where she focuses her research on literacy development, reading difficulties, effective teaching practices for multilingual students, and the implementation of schoolwide systems of support.

Related ASCD Resources

At the time of publication, the following resources were available (ASCD stock numbers appear in parentheses):

Print Products

Team Up, Speak, Up, Fire Up! Educators, Students, and the Community Working Together to Support English Learners by Audrey Cohan, Andrea Honigsfeld, and Maria G. Dove (#120004)

Dispelling Misconceptions About English Language Learners: Research-Based Ways to Improve Instruction by Barbara Gottschalk (#120010)

Success with Multicultural Newcomers &English Learners: Proven Practices for School Leadership Teams by Margarita Espino Calderón and Shawn Slakk (#117026)

Literacy Unleashed: Fostering Excellent Reading Instruction Through Classroom Visits by Bonnie Houck and Sandi Novak (#116042)

Assessing Multilingual Learners: A Month-by-Month Guide by Margo Gottlieb (#SF117076)

How to Reach the Hard to Teach: Excellent Instruction for Those Who Need It Most by Jana Echevarría, Nancy E. Frey, and Douglas Fisher (#116010)

Excellence Through Equity: Five Principles of Courageous Leadership to Guide Achievement for Every Student by Alan M. Blankstein and Pedro Noguera with Lorena Kelly (#116070)

Read, Write, Lead: Breakthrough Strategies for Schoolwide Literacy Success by Regie Routman (#113016)

Classroom Instruction That Works with English Language Learners by Jane D. Hill and Kirsten Miller, 2nd Edition (#114004)

Teaching English Language Learners Across the Content Areas by Judie Haynes and Debbie Zacarian (#109032)

The Language-Rich Classroom: A Research-Based Framework for Teaching English Language Learners by Pérsida Himmele & William Himmele (#108037)

Differentiated Literacy Coaching: Scaffolding for Student and Teacher Success by Mary Catherine Moran (#107053)

Classroom Instruction That Works with English Language Learners Facilitator's Guide by Jane Hill & Cynthia Björk (#108052)

Getting Started with English Language Learners: How Educators Can Meet the Challenge by Judie Haynes (#106048)

Research-Based Methods of Reading Instruction for English Language Learners, Grades K–4 by Sylvia Linan-Thompson and Sharon Vaughn (#108002)

Using Understanding by Design in the Culturally and Linguistically Diverse Classroom by Amy J. Heineke and Jay McTighe (#118084)

10 Success Factors for Literacy Intervention: Getting Results with MTSS in Elementary Schools by Susan L. Hall (#118015)

For up-to-date information about ASCD resources, go to www.ascd.org. You can search the complete archives of *Educational Leadership* at www.ascd.org/el.

ASCD myTeachSource®

Download resources from a professional learning platform with hundreds of research-based best practices and tools for your classroom at http://myteachsource.ascd.org/.

For more information, send an e-mail to member@ascd.org; call 1-800-933-2723 or 703-578-9600; send a fax to 703-575-5400; or write to Information Services, ASCD, 1703 N. Beauregard St., Alexandria, VA 22311-1714 USA.

WHOLE CHILD
TENETS

① **HEALTHY**
Each student enters school healthy and learns about and practices a healthy lifestyle.

② **SAFE**
Each student learns in an environment that is physically and emotionally safe for students and adults.

③ **ENGAGED**
Each student is actively engaged in learning and is connected to the school and broader community.

④ **SUPPORTED**
Each student has access to personalized learning and is supported by qualified, caring adults.

⑤ **CHALLENGED**
Each student is challenged academically and prepared for success in college or further study and for employment and participation in a global environment.

THE WHOLE CHILD

The ASCD Whole Child approach is an effort to transition from a focus on narrowly defined academic achievement to one that promotes the long-term development and success of all children. Through this approach, ASCD supports educators, families, community members, and policymakers as they move from a vision about educating the whole child to sustainable, collaborative actions.

Learning in a New Language relates to the **engaged, supported,** and **challenged** tenets. For more about the ASCD Whole Child approach, visit **www.ascd.org/wholechild.**

LEARN. TEACH. LEAD.